BEADED JEWELRY
⇒ MADE EASY ⇐

BEADED JEWELRY
⋝ MADE EASY ⋜
A Step-by-Step Guide to Making Earrings, Bracelets, Necklaces, and More

LUCY KELLY
CREATOR OF UPCYCLED VINTAGE JEWELRY BRAND BEL MONILI

Skyhorse Publishing

These projects, materials, and tools should not be used by unsupervised children. You will be working with small pieces such as beads and findings that could easily become choking hazards for young children or pets so make sure you safely store these items in a secure container where only an adult can reach. You will be cutting wire or other materials that may become airborne and using some potentially noxious substances such as glues or epoxies so working in a well-ventilated area and wearing a mask, gloves, and protective eyewear are recommended.

Skyhorse Publishing books may be purchased in bulk at special discounts for sales promotion, corporate gifts, fund-raising, or educational purposes. Special editions can also be created to specifications. For details, contact the Special Sales Department, Skyhorse Publishing, 307 West 36th Street, 11th Floor, New York, NY 10018 or info@skyhorsepublishing.com.

Skyhorse® and Skyhorse Publishing® are registered trademarks of Skyhorse Publishing, Inc.®, a Delaware corporation.

Visit our website at www.skyhorsepublishing.com.

10 9 8 7 6 5 4 3 2 1

Library of Congress Cataloging-in-Publication Data is available on file.

Cover design by David Ter-Avanesyan
Cover photo by Lucy Kelly

Print ISBN: 978-1-5107-6832-1
Ebook ISBN: 978-1-5107-6833-8

Printed in China

To the two loves of my life, Erik and Evelyn, everything I am and everything I do is because of your love and support. Erik hung the moon, and Evelyn is our brightly shining star. Thank you.

TABLE OF CONTENTS

PREFACE

• • • • • • • • • • •

I'm going to begin this book with a bold statement: Everyone, everywhere, has at least one piece of jewelry in their possession.

Humans have been adorning themselves since the dawn of time with treasured bits and bobs. If there's one thing that we are all united in, it's surely the love of a good shiny object. Making jewelry is a fun, relaxing, and rewarding activity that anyone can do (yes, you too!). Beaded jewelry in particular lends itself to an endless array of design and style possibilities. You could have one thousand people in one thousand different places follow the directions here in this book, and you will get one thousand completely different works of art.

Jewelry making as a hobby is a wonderful way to engage your mind and your hands in an activity that is both relaxing and productive. One of my favorite aspects of jewelry making is that it doesn't have to be exact or precise, so have fun exploring the different techniques and tools, and don't get too caught up in making sure everything is perfect. There's beauty in rough edges and asymmetries, so make something that brings you joy, and choose colors and textures and combinations to light the little spark inside of you that makes you smile.

Here's a bit of a brief history lesson about me (it's relevant, I promise!). When I

was a school-aged child, my grandmother (I called her Bubbie) had a tiny little antique shop about five to six houses down from my home. We lived in a small suburb of Pittsburgh, the kind of place where everybody knew everybody else, and *someone's* mom was always watching out for what you were doing.

Everyone loved Bubbie's antique shop. It was filled to the brim with beautiful old things: colorful lamps, delicate china with carefully hand-painted designs, well-made wooden furniture pieces, and a continually evolving collection of eclectic jewels. One of the questions she was asked most often was, "How do you decide what to buy?" Her response was invariably, "I buy what I like."

How I loved tagging along with Bubbie when she went on her buying trips! She would carefully evaluate pieces and determine which would be accompanying her back to the shop (or sometimes even to her home). Of course, my very favorite part was when we got to look at the jewelry. The cool, heavy weight of a vintage German glass beaded necklace or the rainbow sparkle of light passing through a perfectly faceted gemstone pendant were notes that resonated with my young heart.

As I grew into an adult and began on my own career path, I found myself drawn to skills that kept my hands busy and my heart full. A couple of jewelry-making classes at a local craft shop taught me the basic skills I needed, and with my newfound knowledge (and some sturdy pliers) I started off on a creative path that has brought me to my own six-figure jewelry and education business.

Sitting in that class, learning the skills of my new hobby, I had no idea what lay ahead. What I did know was that working with beads and making jewelry felt so natural to me and I could do it as much or as little as I liked and be joyful in the activity. This is my wish for you: Whether you are looking to keep your hands busy or you are laying the foundation for your own creative empire, take the time to really enjoy it.

As you are embarking on this creative journey and wondering, *How do I decide what to make?*, I will leave you with a variation on Bubbie's words of wisdom: Make what you like.

CHAPTER 1
JEWELRY-MAKING BASICS

Where to Start

In this book, you will learn about some basic tools and components that are foundational to any jewelry maker's journey. There are infinite possibilities when it comes to beaded jewelry design, which means that you can quickly become overwhelmed with all of the supplies, tools, and options that are out there, so I recommend starting out by seeing what you've already got on hand. That broken necklace, the bracelet that's too short, or the pendant that's pretty but just needs a touch of something else might be the perfect project for you to get started on. Once the word gets out among your family and friends that you are making beaded jewelry, I'll bet you will quickly acquire loads of broken or unwanted pieces to practice with.

Workspace

Jewelry making is a fairly portable hobby, but having a dedicated workspace will make your experience so much easier and more relaxing! Your space doesn't need to be huge, but it should include the following:

- Bright, clean light that allows you to see your work and that doesn't distort colors (this makes a big difference when you are selecting your project components!).
- A clear, hard surface to work on.
- A comfortable, supportive chair.
- If you will be moving from space to space, a lap desk and some sturdy storage boxes will make light work of crafting.
- Since you will be working with small pieces such as beads and head pins, make sure that the space you are working in is safe and clear of clutter so that you can easily see and pick up any loose pieces that make their way off your workspace. Little hands and furry friends have a tendency to find the tiniest of pieces on the floor.

Tools

When it comes to jewelry making, there's a tool for just about everything (and many times there are multiple tools that work together!). Tools range in size, quality, and specialty, so I recommend getting a set of basic all-purpose tools to start out with and upgrading to more professional-grade tools as you hone your craft and develop your design preferences. I personally have come to love my inexpensive rosary pliers and bent-nose pliers, and they have been in my hands as I've created many thousands of pieces of jewelry over the years.

Now, the following items aren't the be-all and end-all list of jewelry-making tools, but before you go on a craft-store shopping spree to buy *all of the tools*, I recommend starting out with these basics. This list of tools and findings, paired with your bead stash, will be enough to get you started and keep you busy for quite some time!

- Beadboard
- Bead mat
- Bent-nose pliers
- Cutters (all-purpose)
- Chain-nose pliers
- Crimping pliers
- Round-nose or rosary pliers (I prefer rosary pliers)
- Ruler
- Scissors

Now, let's learn about some of the different jewelry-making tools you may see and what they are used for:

Beadboard

Beadboards are used to lay out your designs as well as store/organize the components you are using for a project. You can find bead boards for necklaces as well as bracelets, and both varieties are valuable to have on hand when you are designing a project. Many jewelry makers work with the standard gray flocked plastic beadboards, which you can get at any local craft supply store. My personal preference, though, is to work with a heavier and sturdier board that will not crack or spill beads when it is bumped (there are few things as heart-stopping as having your project board go flying everywhere . . . that's a lesson

I only needed to learn once before getting a good board!). My personal favorite bead boards are made by Acclaim Crafts, a husband-and-wife team out of Tennessee. They have a variety of handcrafted bead boards available on their website: www.acclaimcrafts.com.

Beading Needles

Beading needles are thin, flexible needles used for beading a necklace with a cord. These are particularly useful when working with seed beads or small-holed beads such as pearls. I suggest purchasing either a beading cord that has the needle pre-attached or a big-eye beading needle, which can be much easier to thread.

Bead Reamer

A bead reamer is a tool that is used to enlarge and/or smooth the hole of a bead. There are both manual and automatic versions, though I recommend the manual version (reaming beads is gentle work!).

Cutters

Cutters are essential for your jewelry-making toolbox. You want to have at least one sturdy multipurpose cutter, and if you are using harder wires such as memory wire (which will nick the edges of your regular cutters), you will want to have a dedicated pair of heavy-duty cutters as well. The most common varieties of cutters include:

- **Flat cutters:** Flat cutters are designed to cut wire, with the blade on the top edge of the tool. These are useful when you need to cut right up against a flat surface.
- **Flush cutters:** Flush cutters are designed to cut wire, with the blade on the angled side of the tool. These will cut a straight edge across the wire, leaving a flat end.
- **Heavy-duty cutters:** Heavy-duty cutters are specifically designed for harder wires such as memory wire. It's important to have a dedicated pair of pliers specifically for your harder wires because those can easily nick or damage the edges of traditional cutters.
- **Side cutters:** Side cutters, also known as angle cutters, are designed to cut an angled edge across the wire, leaving an angled end.

Knotting Tool/Awl

A knotting tool is used to form knots between beads that are strung on a cord (usually silk or nylon). Some jewelry makers use a traditional awl, while others prefer a specialty knotting tool to use both hands while knotting. In this book, I show you how to use an awl to create your knots. Once you are comfortable with the technique, try using the specialty knotting tool to see which method you prefer.

Pliers

As you start making jewelry, you will quickly find a handful (no pun intended!) of favorite pliers to work with. Many of these can be used interchangeably. I personally prefer to work with both bent-nose pliers and rosary pliers for the majority of my beaded jewelry projects.

- **Bent-nose/curved-nose pliers:** Bent-nose/curved-nose pliers have a curved tip that makes them perfect for getting into tight spaces, and the flat interior sides make it easier for them to grip materials such as wire and beads. The curve of the pliers makes them ideal for opening and closing jump rings and holding an eye-pin end straight.
- **Bracelet-bending pliers:** Bracelet-bending pliers have two slightly crescent-shaped plates, usually made from nylon, that allow you to manually bend a piece of metal into a consistent curve to make a bracelet.
- **Chain-nose pliers:** Chain-nose pliers have a flat end and are used for gripping and manipulating wire, head pins, and eye pins. These are also a good option for opening and closing jump rings and the like.
- **Crimping pliers:** Crimping pliers are used to close and secure crimp beads and crimp tubes and close a crimp cover bead. This multipurpose tool will be a workhorse in your toolbox.
- **Jump-ring/split-ring pliers:** Jump-ring/split-ring pliers have one straight tip and one bent tip that allows you to open up a jump/split ring and attach to other findings.
- **Nylon-jaw pliers:** Nylon-jaw pliers are designed for shaping wire and for wire wrapping. The nylon coating protects the wire from nicks and gouges that come from metal-on-metal contact and allows you to manipulate the wire without making excessive crimps or dents.
- **Rosary pliers:** Rosary pliers are a staple in my jewelry-making repertoire. They have the same conical tips as round-nose pliers but have a cutter built in above the handle that makes rosary-style beading (beading on eye pins to connect and create a beaded chain) quick and easy.
- **Round-nose pliers:** Round-nose pliers have two rounded ends that are designed to make looping and bending easier. The cone shape of the plier's tips allows you to make different sized loops (smaller if you wrap toward the tip and larger if you wrap toward the base).

Ring Mandrel

A ring mandrel is a cone-shaped tool, usually crafted from stainless steel or plastic, that allows you to create, reshape, or size/resize rings. If you are using wire to create rings, a plastic mandrel will be preferable to avoid metal-on-metal nicks and dings.

Tweezers

Tweezers are an excellent multipurpose tool to have in your jewelry-making toolbox because they can help you pick up and manipulate tiny components that are difficult to manage with your fingertips. Varieties include straight-tipped, slant-tipped, serrated, and bent-nose tweezers.

Findings

Findings are the components used to create and assemble jewelry. They come in a spectrum of styles, sizes, and finishes. Accents such as filigrees, bead caps, spacers, and charms add interest and unique style to any beaded jewelry design, while eye pins, head pins, and wire are the foundational components of many beaded jewelry pieces.

PRO TIP

When selecting findings and chain to work with, choose one finish to start out with (i.e., if you like an antiqued silver finish, purchase your chain, head pins, eye pins, ear wires, etc., all in an antiqued silver finish). This is going to give your finished jewelry pieces a much more cohesive look, and it is going to be friendlier to your wallet!

Here is an overview of the most common types of jewelry findings:

- **Bails:** Bails are used to attach a pendant to a necklace. Some bails have a loop at the bottom to attach with a ring, while others can be glued or attached directly to a stone or pendant.
- **Bead caps:** Bead caps are decorative pieces that are strung next to beads to create a specialized, embellished look. These come in a variety of sizes and are designed to fit snugly up against a bead of the same size.

- **Bead cord:** Bead cord is usually composed of silk or nylon and is used to string or knot beads. There are a variety of thicknesses and colors to choose from. Thinner cord is preferable for smaller holed/lighter beads such as pearls, while thicker cord is used for larger holed/heavier beads such as glass or stone.
- **Bead spacers:** Bead spacers are flat beads that are strung in between other larger beads to add interest and flexibility to the jewelry piece. They are made from a variety of materials, most often metal, plastic, or stone.
- **Bead wire:** Beading wire is used to string beads and comes in a variety of thicknesses and qualities. The strand count of beading wire indicates the number of individual wires that are twisted together and coated in nylon to form the beading wire. This wire traditionally comes in 7-strand, 19-strand, 21-strand, and 49-strand varieties. The higher the strand count, the more flexible (and stronger) the wire will be. When you are learning/practicing, 7-strand wire is a great inexpensive option to practice with. Once you are comfortable, though, I recommend working with at least 21-strand (I personally work with 49-strand for all of my designs).
- **Chains:** There are hundreds of different types of chains to choose from, but here are a few of the most common types to work with when creating beaded jewelry:
  - **Ball chain:** A series of round beads that are connected, usually made of a base metal such as stainless steel or brass.
  - **Cable chain:** A basic chain style composed of uniform oval links that are connected.
  - **Curb chain:** A curb chains usually has a heavy, chunky appearance. It lays flat against the wearer's skin and is composed of uniform links that are connected and flattened.
  - **Figaro chain:** A more decorative chain, usually with two to three smaller round links and one larger link that are attached in a repeating pattern.
  - **Rope chain:** Another common chain style composed of metal links that are twisted around one other to create a rope-like appearance.
- **Charms:** Charms come in all shapes and sizes, in just about any design or theme you could imagine. They are usually made from metal or molded plastic metal. You can also create your own charms using beads on a head pin.
- **Clamps:** Clamps are used to create a finished end to a soft material such as ribbon or leather. It has two edges with "teeth" that are clamped closed over the end of the material with a loop that allows it to be attached to a jump ring or chain.
- **Clamshell knot ends:** Clamshell knot ends (also called fold-over bead tips) are used with bead cord to cover up the knot at the end of the necklace and create a

finished look. The knot "hides" in the cup of the clamshell while a loop allows it to be connected to a jump ring or clasp.

- **Clasps**
  - **Barrel clasps:** Composed of two barrel-shaped pieces that screw together to close.
  - **Fold-over clasp:** A hinged clasp that hooks over a loop and snaps to form a closure.
  - **Hook-and-eye clasps:** Hook-and-eye clasps have a hook that loops through a ring or loop (the "eye") to form a closure.
  - **Lobster-claw clasp:** A teardrop-shaped clasp with a tiny lever and spring that opens and closes the clasp.
  - **Magnetic clasps:** Magnetic clasps have a strong magnet on each side and are great for people who have arthritis or difficulty manipulating small objects.
  - **Spring-ring clasp:** A circular clasp with a tiny lever and spring that opens and closes the clasp (similar to a lobster claw).
  - **Toggle clasp:** A bar that slips through a loop. Many toggle clasps are decorative and used as the focal/pendant part of the piece as an interesting design twist.
- **Craft wire:** Craft wire comes in many different materials, gauges (sizes), and finishes. Smaller gauge numbers are thicker wire, while larger gauge numbers are thinner wire.
- **Cones:** A cone finding is used to finish off the end of a multi-strand necklace, bringing all the strands of the necklace together through this single piece.
- **Cord:** Cord is a term used to describe any material that can be used for stringing, which is most often leather, ribbon, silk, velvet, or hemp.
- **Crimp beads/crimp tubes:** Crimp beads and tubes are used to finish the ends of a beaded piece (usually on bead wire) to secure the finished piece together.
- **Crimp covers:** Crimp covers are c-shaped flexible open metal beads used to cover a finished crimp tube or bead. Crimp covers close over the top of the crimp to create the look of a metal bead (hiding the finished crimp).
- **Earring findings**
  - **Clip-on earring findings:** Clip-ons most often have a hinge with a padded arm that allows someone to wear the earring without having pierced ears.
  - **Posts:** There are a variety of different post styles, including ball posts, cup pads, and flat pads. Ball posts have a decorative ball and a loop to attach a finding or bead. Cup pads have a cupped peg for attaching a bead or round

finding. Flat pads have a flat peg for attaching to the back of something flat, like a cabochon.

- **French wires:** French wires are hooks that slip through and hang from the ear and can be worn with or without wire keepers (small rubber or plastic stoppers that keep the earring in place).
- **Hoops:** Hoops are wire circles that can either serve as the complete finding itself or can be attached to another type of ear wire.
- **Kidney wire:** Kidney-shaped wire has a small hook on the back that the end of the wire tucks into to stay secure in the ear.
- **Leverbacks:** Leverbacks have a short hook that loops through the earlobe and a hinged back that closes over the tip of the wire in the back.
- **Elastic:** Elastic is a stretch cord that is used for beading (usually bracelets) and is available in different colors and diameters. There are uncoated and nylon-coated varieties. The uncoated elastic is smoother and thinner, while the nylon-coated is thicker and better suited for larger holed/heavier beads.
- **Eye pin:** An eye pin is a straight piece of metal wire with a prefabricated loop on one end. Eye pins come in a variety of lengths, gauges, and finishes.
- **Filigrees:** Filigrees are decorative pieces of stamped metal that are used to add interest and style to jewelry pieces. These come in an endless variety of shapes and sizes and can be bent, rolled, painted, or even cut to create a truly unique look.
- **Glues:** Glues are a wonderful and easy way to attach jewelry components, but please be sure to heed the instructions and safety precautions on the product packaging.
- **Superglue:** Superglue is a multipurpose glue that can be used to bond everything from metal to glass to plastic.
  - **Epoxy:** Epoxy is usually a two-part glue system that must be mixed at the time it will be used (i.e., you can't pre-mix and save it).
  - **E-6000:** E-6000 is another good multipurpose adhesive that works well on a variety of materials. It dries to a sturdy and flexible finish.
- **Head pin:** A head pin is a straight piece of metal wire with a flat head on one end, typically used for creating pendants or bead drops. Head pins come in a variety of finishes and lengths.
- **Jump ring:** A jump ring is a metal loop that opens to attach jewelry elements to one another. Jump rings are most often circular or oval and come in a variety of sizes, gauges, and finishes.

- **Memory wire:** Memory wire is a thin, hard wire that is formed into a spring and retains its shape even after adding beads and jewelry elements. It comes in different sizes for bracelets, necklaces, and even rings. This wire is very hard and should be cut with dedicated heavy-duty cutters.
- **Multi-strand ends:** Multi-strand ends allow you to create necklaces or bracelets that have multiple strands of beads or even chandelier-style earrings with multiple drops.
- **Pin backs:** Pin backs can be attached to the back of elements such as a cabochon or flat-backed filigree to create a brooch.
- **Spacer bars:** Spacer bars are thin bars of metal or resin with holes that are used to hold multiple strand necklaces or bracelets in line.
- **Split rings:** Split rings look like tiny key rings, with overlapping wire loops that can be opened with your fingernail (or, much better, with a split ring tool).
- **Wire:** Wire comes in a variety of colors, materials, and sizes. Wire thickness is measured in gauges, with smaller numbers equating to larger thicknesses. It is used to create stand-alone elements or to wrap around beads or findings to add visual interest.
- **Wire protector:** Wire protectors fall under the "nice to have" category of findings. They are used to thread your wire through to protect it from the wear and tear of rubbing against clasps, jump rings, or other sharp finding edges.

Storage

With that long list of supplies, you are going to need a secure and safe way to store everything. Look for storage containers that are see-through and offer sectioned compartments. Ideally, your storage container will have a lid with separations/seals that close securely over each section of the compartment so that a drop or bump doesn't send your beads flying all over the container. Some brands offer locking lids, which are useful for keeping small beads in and small hands out. Containers that are stackable/nestable are going to make it easier for you to store, sort, and organize your beads and findings. It's also a good idea to separate your findings from your beads when you are storing them to make it easier for you to quickly find what you are looking for (and what you may need to replenish).

Pro Tip
Storage containers that have compartments with curved or rounded bottom edges make it much easier to get beads or findings out!

Nice-to-Have Accessories

Once you get the basics of jewelry making down pat and you start to discover your favorite materials and techniques, these little extras can really come in handy:

- **Bead stoppers:** Bead stoppers are tiny springs with a little finger pad at each end that allow you to open up the spring, place the end of a beading wire through it, and hold beads in place on a strand. This little gadget is particularly useful when you are working on multi-strand bead projects or when working with elastic.
- **Extra sets of your favorite tools:** I learned this one the hard way. When you find pliers or other tools that you absolutely love to work with, keep a spare on hand! Jewelry tools don't last forever, and it's a little heartbreaking to be in the middle of a project and have to stop because your pliers broke.
- **Extra hand or third hand:** An "extra hand" tool is a weighted arm that has clamps on either end that allow you to secure a piece while you work on it. This is especially useful when you are adding multiple beads or charms to a chain.
- **Ring mandrel:** A ring mandrel allows you to make, size, and shape a ring. Mandrels are typically made of metal or hard plastic. Many people who make rings like to have both versions, but the hard plastic version will prevent nicks and scratches from metal-on-metal contact when making wire-wrapped rings.
- **Ring sizing tool:** This tool allows you to measure the size of any finger.
- **Rubber mallet:** A small rubber mallet can be useful for flattening wire, shaping metal, and sizing/resizing rings on a mandrel. Be sure to choose a mallet with a soft rubber or nylon head that is specifically designed for jewelry making.
- **Tool stand:** A tool stand is a plastic or acrylic stand that lets you store all your pliers in one place. This is nice to have when you are working with many different tools.
- **Wire jig:** A wire jig is a board with different-sized holes where you can place pegs to form a pattern, then wrap wire around the pegs to make loops, findings, and fun accent pieces. This is a nice piece to have if you decide you want to get into more intricate wire designs or stand-alone wire focal pieces.

Gift Packaging

Once you get comfortable with beaded jewelry making, you may find yourself wanting to gift some of your lovely work. When selecting your packaging, be sure to choose materials that will cushion, protect, and even enhance the gift that's inside. Acid-free tissue paper can be used to wrap your pieces safely. If you will be sending a beaded creation in the mail, take care to wrap the piece in tissue, bubble wrap, or both before sending it on its way. Gift boxes that come with a batting liner are relatively inexpensive and come in a wide variety of sizes and shapes to accommodate different project sizes. You want to select a size that your finished design will fit into snugly so that it doesn't slide around (and potentially get damaged).

Where to Shop

There are *so* many different places to purchase supplies. Where should you go to get yours? The easiest and most obvious answer is your local craft supply store. These stores are easily accessible and have all the basic items you need to get started on your beaded jewelry-making journey. As a bonus, many of them offer regular discounts and coupons that will save you some money (fair warning: bead buying is addictive and can get expensive quickly!). Many large retailers also offer crafting sections that are stocked with basic beaded jewelry-making supplies. These would be good places to go if you are looking for materials to practice with.

Did you know that "bead shows" are a thing? Bead shows are a great way to see (and learn about) a huge variety of beads, findings, tools, and extras all in one place. Sellers at these shows are well-versed in their materials and will take the time to tell you about their products. Think of them as a sort of convention for beaded jewelry makers. They are usually two to three days long and take place at hotels or convention centers. A quick Google search for "bead shows near (insert your city's name here)" will let you know if there are any upcoming bead shows in your area.

Once you know which materials you want, Amazon is a great option for quick, easy, affordable supplies. I will caution you here that purchasing beads and findings online can be tricky, though. Be sure you carefully read the description of the sizes and quantities of what you are buying. Sometimes what looks tiny on the screen can show up being the size of your hand, and vice versa!

When you have mastered your techniques and are ready to expand your horizons, there are many websites that are dedicated to beads, findings, and jewelry-making supplies. Here are a few of my favorites:

Acclaim Crafts: www.acclaimcrafts.com
Artbeads: www.artbeads.com
Etsy: www.etsy.com
Fire Mountain Gems: www.firemountaingems.com
Rings & Things: www.rings-things.com
Rio Grande: www.riogrande.com

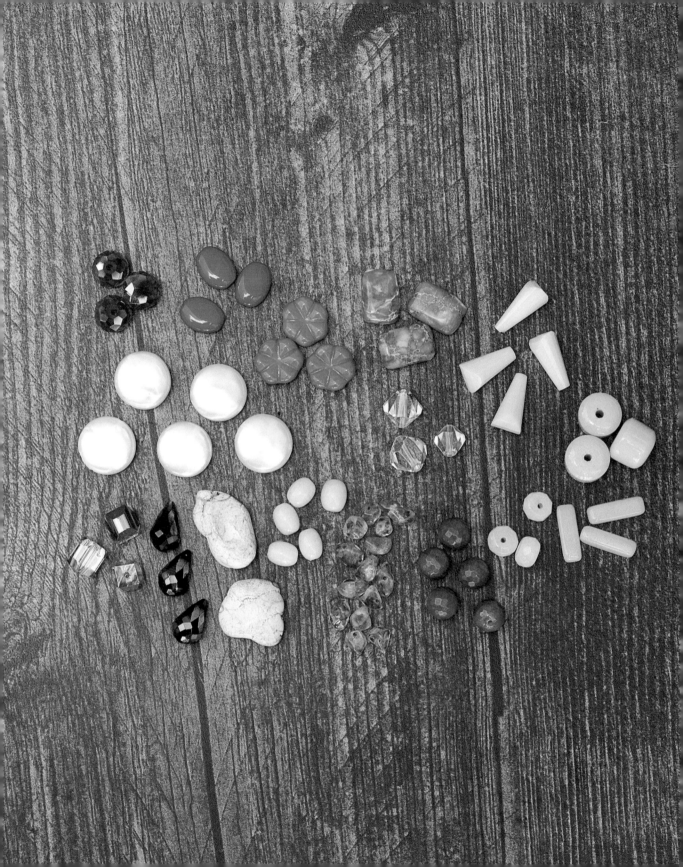

Chapter 2
ALL ABOUT BEADS

············

Bead Sizes

Beads come in all different sizes and are generally measured by diameter. The most common sizes for jewelry making are 4mm, 6mm, 8mm, 10mm, and 12mm. I like to use 1mm–2mm beads as spacers, and larger beads (14mm+) to make great pendants. When you are designing projects that are strung on bead wire, remember that the larger the bead is, the less flexible the necklace will be. As a rule of thumb, I personally like to use spacers in between beads that are 6mm or larger to ensure that my finished design is flexible and hangs nicely. Beads are typically sold in 8"–16" strands. Shorter strands can often be found at your local craft store, and longer strands are more commonly found at bead shows or in bulk amounts. If you are purchasing wholesale or in bulk, beads are sometimes sold by weight. Be sure you understand how many beads will be in each strand/order so that you are sure to purchase enough to complete your project. There are always things you can make with leftover beads!

Bead Styles and Shapes

There is a seemingly endless array of bead shapes. (If you can drill a hole in it, it can be a bead!) This is where we really get into the fun of beaded jewelry making. Here are a few of the most common bead styles and shapes:

- Bicone
- Briolette
- Chip
- Coin
- Cone
- Cube
- Drop
- Faceted
- Lentil
- Nugget
- Oval
- Rectangle
- Rondelle
- Round
- Triangle
- Tube/Cylinder

Bead Hole Sizes and Drill Types

Bead hole sizes range from bead to bead. When selecting your stringing material, it's important to account for the size of the hole in the beads you are working with. Natural pearls tend to have smaller holes and require thinner wire or silk thread. Larger stone, glass, or lampwork beads tend to have larger holes that could be strung on a thicker material such as cord or wire. When purchasing beads, especially online, be sure you know the diameter of the bead hole so that you know what stringing material will work best for your project.

There are also variations on how holes can be drilled into a bead. When looking at and thinking of beads, we most often think of them with a hole drilled directly down the middle of the longest part, which is called center-drilled. A similar variation of the center-drilled bead is vertical-drilled, in which the bead has a clear visual top and bottom (such as a shaped bead), and the hole is drilled straight through the center of the bead from the top to the bottom. Large or oddly shaped beads (such as a teardrop shape) are sometimes drilled either front to back (front-drilled) or side to side (side-drilled) if they are intended to be used as a pendant.

Bead Weights

The weight of a bead is directly dependent on the size and material. Plastic and shell beads are more lightweight than metal, glass, or stone beads. When you are creating your jewelry, make sure to account for the weight of the finished project and how comfortable it will be to wear. You also want to be sure that the findings you choose are strong enough to support the weight of the beads and the finished piece. Thin wires will bend or break under the heavy weight of stones or glass.

Bead Materials

Beads come in an endless variety of materials, which is another reason why they are so fun to work with! The most common materials include clay, glass, natural stone, and plastic. Working with beads of different materials, shapes, and sizes allows you to really get creative with your jewelry designs and make pieces that are truly unique. Here are some of the most frequently used bead types (use this as a guide to spark ideas about which materials you might want to use in your designs!):

- **Ceramic beads:** Ceramic beads are created from ceramic (or porcelain) and usually have a glazed or painted finish.
- **Clay beads:** Polymer clay is a popular material to work with in jewelry making. It is lightweight, easy to work with, and can be cured/finished without needing a kiln. These beads can be any shape or size.
- **Crystal beads:** Crystal beads are made from glass or natural rock crystal that is machine cut and then polished to create a beautiful sparkle. Genuine crystal glass is created using glass that contains a percentage of lead, which gives it that extra special shine.

- **Glass beads:** Glass beads come in an endless variety of shapes, sizes, and colors. Varieties of glass beads include colorful African trade beads, richly colored Czech glass beads, sparkly dichroic glass beads, handmade lampwork glass beads, and even tiny seed beads.
- **Metal beads:** Metal beads can be made with a variety of metals including brass, copper, pewter, and stainless steel. These beads make excellent textural accents to mix with natural stone and can stand alone in a statement piece.
- **Pearls:** Pearls are widely used in jewelry design and come in several varieties:
  - Glass pearls have a glass core and are coated with a paint or lacquer that gives them a pearl-like finish.
  - Freshwater pearls are created by seeding a freshwater mollusk. They can be farmed in different shapes and sizes and can be naturally colored (usually a creamy white) or can be dyed for a unique look.
  - Cultured pearls are created by seeding a saltwater oyster and are usually round in shape. These are considered to be much higher quality than freshwater or glass pearls.
- **Plastic beads:** Plastic beads come in a wide variety of shapes, colors, and sizes and are very lightweight. Many vintage plastic beads were created using Bakelite or Lucite, while more modern plastic beads are created by molding regular plastic into a bead shape.
- **Shell beads:** Shell beads are created from many different kinds of shells and can be shaped, polished, or even dyed for unique finishes.
- **Stone beads:** Stone beads are created using natural stone materials that are cut, shaped, and finished to create truly unique beads. Semiprecious gemstone beads have beautiful designs, patterns, and textures that are a natural feature of these materials. Some stones, like quartz and agate, can be dyed or coated for additional variety.
- **Wood beads:** Wooden beads (sometimes also created using nut husks) are lightweight and easy to work with. They can be easily carved or painted. Due to the light weight of this material, large-sized wooden or nut beads can be used to make a nice statement piece.

Beyond this list is a sea of bead materials that are waiting to be discovered. If you're feeling adventurous, take a spin around your jewelry box and see if there are any pieces that you just don't love anymore . . . you could be your own source of beads before going all-in on your new bead-buying habit!

CHAPTER 3
BASIC TECHNIQUES AND DESIGN TIPS

When you are getting started, there are a few basic techniques that are foundational to all jewelry designs. Practice these techniques before you start working on any major projects and give yourself time to learn and improve. As with any skill, the more you practice, the easier it will be (and the better the finished product will look).

Opening and Closing Jump Rings and Loops

When opening a jump ring or any other split loop, it is important to use tools and proper techniques to ensure that the integrity of the shape and the strength of the ring are maintained. You will always open with a front-to-back parallel twisting movement.

TOOLS

- Bent-nose pliers
- Jump ring or other open-loop finding
- Rosary/round-nose pliers

Step 1: Using the flat edge of your bent-nose pliers, grasp the jump ring so that the opening is parallel with the tip of your pliers.

Step 2: With your rosary or round-nose pliers, grasp the other side of the jump ring and twist your left hand toward you and your right hand away from you, opening the ring perpendicularly.

Step 3: Loop the jump ring through the findings or components that you will be attaching together.

Step 4: Grasping the jump ring in the same manner, twist the jump ring back into place, ensuring that the ends meet flush and that there is no gap between the ends.

Making Loops

TOOLS

- Beads
- Bead wire
- Head pin or eye pin
- Bent-nose pliers
- Cutters (all-purpose)
- Rosary pliers or round-nose pliers

Step 1: Stack the beads on the wire in your chosen pattern. Use your thumb and forefinger to hold the beads together, pushed against the head of the head pin or the eye of the eye pin.

Step 2: Using your other hand or a pair of bent-nose pliers, bend the end of the wire down just past a 90° angle.

Step 3: Using your cutters, leave about 1cm (you can approximate using the length of your pinky nail bed) and cut off the excess wire.

Step 4: Grasp the end of the wire with the rosary pliers and roll the wire all the way around the tip, bringing the end of the wire back to the base of the pin to form a closed loop.

Alternative Finish: Wire Wrapping

Instead of cutting off the excess wire (see Step 3 of Making Loops on previous page), some people prefer to wrap the end of the wire around the stem for a decorative (and more secure) effect. This finish is particularly useful when your beads are heavier and need more support.

Step 1: Stack the beads on the wire in your chosen pattern. Use your thumb and forefinger to hold the beads together, pushed against the head of the head pin or the eye of the eye pin. Leaving about ½" of wire below the bend, use your other hand (or a pair of pliers) to bend the end of the wire down just past a 90° angle.

Step 2: Grasp the wire with your rosary pliers just above the bend and roll the wire around the nose of the pliers, leaving the long tail of the wire sticking out to the side.

Step 3: Using the pliers to hold the loop in place, use your other hand to wrap the end of the wire around the stem, below the loop.

Step 4: Use the tip of your bent-nose pliers to shape the end of the wire into place, creating a smooth edge to the wrap.

Stringing

Flexible beading wire is a strong and secure stringing material that will allow you to create pieces of varying lengths and weights. Beading wire comes in a variety of diameters, strengths, and colors. They are made by weaving together stainless steel strands that are then nylon coated for strength and durability. When choosing a wire to work with, it's important to remember that the higher the strand count, the stronger (and more flexible) the wire will be. The most common varieties are 7-strand, 19-strand, 21-strand, and 49-strand. 49-strand bead wire is the strongest, most flexible wire option and is the best choice for a beautiful drape and finish to your beaded project. Beading wire accommodates the many different hole sizes of beads. Smaller diameter wires are best for small-holed or lightweight beads, such as pearls (and can even be knotted), while larger diameter wires are best for larger-holed or heavier beads. When using beading wire, you will use crimp tubes to secure the ends of the piece.

Crimping

Crimp beads or tubes are used to secure the ends of your piece, giving it a strong finish to make sure that it will be durable for wear. When selecting your crimp bead or tube, choose the one that coordinates with the diameter of the bead wire you choose.

Wire diameter	Crimp tube/bead diameter
0.026" (0.66mm)	0.052" (1.32mm)
0.024" (0.61mm)	0.048" (1.22mm)
0.020" (0.51mm)	0.040" (1.02mm)
0.019" (0.48mm)	0.038" (0.97mm)
0.015" (0.38mm)	0.030" (0.76mm)
0.014" (0.36mm)	0.028" (0.71mm)
0.012" (0.30mm)	0.024" (0.61mm)
0.0095" (0.24mm)	0.019" (0.48mm)
0.0083" (0.21mm)	0.017" (0.43mm)
0.0070" (0.18mm)	0.014" (0.36mm)

Many brands of bead wire will give you a guide on the packaging to indicate what size bead or tube goes with that wire, making it much easier for you to know that you are using the correct components!

Stringing with Bead Wire

TOOLS

- Bead wire
- Beads
- Crimp tube/bead
- Jump ring/clasp
- Crimp pliers
- Cutters (all-purpose)

Step 1: Pull out a length of bead wire (I prefer to work with 8"–10" at a time, leaving the wire attached to the spool to add more as I use it) and string your beads on. After all of the beads are on the wire, slide the crimp tube or bead onto the end of the wire. Loop the end of the wire through the component you are attaching it to (i.e, a jump ring, a clasp, etc.). Run the wire back through the crimp tube or bead, leaving a tail of approximately ½mm to tuck into the end bead (this makes for a smoother finish to the piece and leaves no rough or scratchy edges).

Step 2: Using the crimp pliers, place the crimp in the kidney bean-shaped position inside of the pliers (closest to your hand). Squeeze the pliers to close the tube or bead, creating a kidney shape to the crimp.

Step 3: Move the tube or bead to the outer circle-shaped position of the pliers (closest to the tip) and turn the crimp ¼ turn so that the groove is facing outward (like a backward "c"). Squeeze the pliers again to flatten the crimp, rounding it out nicely and creating a strong hold on the wire.

Crimp Covers

Crimp covers are an extra step, but they really go a long way to create a beautiful, finished look to your design. Crimp covers are c-shaped open beads that clamp over your finished crimp. Using the end opening of your crimp pliers, gently squeeze down on the crimp cover to close it and give it the look of a finished metal bead. I suggest using crimp covers that are the same color/finish as your other findings to create a cohesive look to your design.

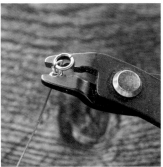

Stringing with Thread/Cord

There are several different types of bead thread/cord, with the most common types being silk and nylon. When stringing beads with cord, many jewelry makers will place a knot in between each bead for strength and security. If you are working with pearls, precious stones, or delicate materials such as glass, it is a good idea to add a knot in between the beads for extra protection. As with other projects, I suggest you practice this technique first with an inexpensive nylon cord while you are learning to hone your skills. As you get better with the technique, you can move into higher quality materials.

TOOLS

- Scissors
- Beading cord of choice
- Beading needle
- Clamshell knot cover connector
- Superglue (optional)
- Bent-nose pliers
- Rosary pliers or round-nose pliers
- Beads
- Knotting tool or awl
- Jump ring
- Clasp

Step 1: With your scissors, cut a length of cord at least 4x the desired length of your project. At one end of the cord, tie a tight knot about ½"–1" away from the end. If your cord is thin, you may choose to tie multiple knots. Slide the other end of the cord through the beading needle. Slide the needle through the clamshell knot cover connector so that the knot rests inside the cup.

(Optional: Add a dot of superglue on the knot here for extra security).

Step 2: Using the flat edge of your bent-nose pliers, squeeze the clamshell closed. Then, use the tip of your rosary pliers or round-nose pliers to close the loop on the end of the connector.

Step 3: Slide a bead onto the cord. Loosely tie a knot in the cord close to the bead. Using your knotting tool or awl, slide the knot down so it's right next to the bead. Pull out the knotting tool or awl and tighten the knot. Repeat these steps until your piece is as long as you'd like it to be. When you've added the last bead, slide the needle

through the bottom side of a second clamshell knot cover connector. Tie a knot (you may need to tie 2 to 3 knots if your thread is thin), using your knotting tool or awl to keep the knot and knot cover close to the end bead. Trim any excess cord once the clamshell is securely closed. Attach a jump ring at one end and a clasp at the other end of the piece.

Stringing with Elastic

Elastic is fun to work with when creating beaded bracelets. I suggest starting out with a simple single strand of beads, eventually working your way up to more complex multi-strand pieces with unique focal pieces and finishes. Elastic cord comes in different diameters and colors. For most projects, 0.7mm elastic will be your best choice, but 1mm elastic is the best all-purpose elastic to use for beads that are heavy and/or have a large hole. I prefer to use Stretch Magic brand clear 0.7mm elastic, but I encourage you to test different brands and finishes to see what works best for you.

TOOLS

- Beading elastic of choice
- Beads
- Scissors
- Superglue (optional)
- Bent-nose pliers

Step 1: Pull out a length of elastic that's approximately twice the length of your wrist, leaving it attached to the spool, and pre-stretch the elastic. String your beads onto the elastic,

leaving approximately 2" of elastic at the end. With your scissors, trim the elastic off of the spool, leaving 2" on the other end. Using a surgeon's knot (two overhand twists in one direction and one overhand twist in the other direction), tightly tie the two ends together. (Optional: Dab a tiny dot of superglue on the knot for extra security.) Trim the excess ends. If possible, use the tip of your bent-nose pliers to tuck the knot inside of a bead hole to cover and protect it.

> **Pro Tip**
> Pre-stretching the elastic ensures that your bracelet will have enough beads on it to completely encircle the wrist without any gaps once it's put on. Plus, it prevents the cord from stretching more over time and altering the fit of the bracelet.

Design

Now, *this* is where you really get to have some fun! Working with beads gives you an endless buffet of colors, sizes, shapes, textures, and finishes to work with. One of the best things about jewelry making is that there are very few "rules" when it comes to design. There are, however, a few things to keep in mind when you are creating your pieces.

Material Choice

When creating a piece or a collection of beaded jewelry, it is important to plan out your projects to make sure you have enough beads to complete all the pieces you want to include. It's also important to make sure that the materials complement one another in size, color, quality, and finish. I suggest selecting one element or feature that is the same among all the varieties that will be included in your pieces. For example, if you are working with natural gemstones, variations in design could look like:

- The same stone type with different sizes, shapes, or finishes
- Different stone types in colors adjacent on the color wheel with the same size, shape, or finish
- Different stone types in all different colors with the same size, shape, and finish

The key here is to have one design element that brings the entire piece or collection together, a subtle yet important factor in designing beautifully beaded jewelry.

Color Combinations

Another beautiful thing about making beaded jewelry is that there are absolutely no limits to what you can design! When I began my jewelry-making journey back in 2010, one of the things I quickly became known for was my unique color combinations. I love unexpected yet lovely pairings such as bubblegum pink with cherry red or bright turquoise with a tart punch of tangerine. If selecting color combinations isn't your forte, there are lots of places you can go to find inspiration. A peek into your closet will give you some good insight on what colors you gravitate toward. Selecting beads that are complementary (within the same color palette) or contrasting (opposite on the color wheel) is also a great place to start. Another great source of color inspiration is the home improvement store. Yes, you read that correctly. Take a walk down the paint aisle and pick up some of those pre-coordinated paint brochures. You will see how the designer coordinated palettes of hues that create a beautiful, harmonized design. You can't go wrong with a good old-fashioned online Pinterest search for color palettes. Searching for things like "modern color palette," "spring color palette," and the like will yield an endless array of expertly paired colors to help you choose your bead colors.

"Bead Soup"

"Bead soup" (sometimes also called "kitchen sink") is a phrase commonly used by beaders to describe any project that uses up all of your leftover beads. The result is a wild mix of colors, shapes, sizes, and textures in a genuinely one-of-a-kind piece. Choose your project depending on how many beads you have and how many pieces you want to create. Any of the projects in this book would be great "bead soup" projects.

Scale

If you've ever looked at a piece of jewelry and thought to yourself, *There's something wrong here, but I'm not quite sure what it is*, I'd bet dollars to doughnuts that the scale was off. For the purposes of designing beaded jewelry, the scale of the piece is the size and shape of the beads relative to one another and to the length of the piece. When designing your own beaded jewelry, a general rule of thumb is to use the smaller beads toward the ends of the piece, gradually moving to the larger beads in the center of the piece. This is not only visually appealing, but it also allows the piece to hang properly. (Think of how difficult it would be to get a necklace with large beads at the back of the neck and small beads at the center to stay in place!) You also want to consider the size of the bead relative to the piece you are creating. Necklaces and bracelets can be designed with larger, chunkier beads because there is more length to work with, while beads for earrings tend to be smaller and more lightweight. The findings and other components in the piece should be similar to the beads. Tiny findings paired with large beads make for an awkward finished product, and vice versa.

Comfort

If you're going to spend all this time and energy creating beautiful pieces of jewelry, you definitely want to make sure they are wearable! Necklaces should drape naturally and lay flat across the chest, earrings should be relatively lightweight, and bracelets should be a bit sturdier (since they will come into contact with more surfaces like keyboards and tabletops). I suggest you "test wear" each item you make to get an idea of how comfortable it is. Pay attention to things like how easy the clasp is to manipulate, how the item is lying/draping, and how often you need to move or adjust it while it's being worn.

CHAPTER 4
EARRINGS

· · · · · · · · · · ·

Earrings are a fun, quick, satisfying way to start out making beaded jewelry. Using a few of the techniques you learned in Chapter 3 on page 16, experiment with all different types of findings, beads, and finishes in this chapter to create an endless wardrobe of handcrafted ear candy!

EAR WIRE TYPES

In Chapter 1 on page 8, you learned about a few of the most commonly used ear wire types. For the projects in this chapter, we will be using French hooks, posts, leverbacks, and kidney wires. Feel free to switch around between different types of wires from project to project. The sky's the limit!

TECHNIQUES

The techniques needed to complete the projects in this chapter include opening and closing jump rings, making loops, and stringing. Refer back to these techniques in Chapter 3 on page 16 when working through these projects.

Design Variations

- Add decorative bead spacers between beads for a more dramatic design.
- Use a jump ring to cluster together several drops, making a cha-cha style earring.
- Test different lengths with different ear wires. A simple single bead dangle can be demure on a post or dramatic on a large hoop.

SIMPLE BEADED DROP EARRINGS

These simple beaded drop earrings are a staple in any accessory wardrobe, and the design possibilities are endless. Making a pair of these earrings is the perfect project to start with, especially if you have a collection of beautiful one-off beads that are waiting to be used.

MATERIALS TO GATHER
- Beads
- Head pins
- Ear wires

TOOLS
- Bead mat/rimmed tray for materials
- Rosary pliers

MAKE IT!

Step 1: Lay out your design, then place your beads in your desired order on the head pin. Holding the beads down to the bottom "head" of the pin in one hand, use the other hand to bend the end of the head-pin wire down just past a 90° angle.

Step 2: Leaving about ¼" of wire next to the bead, use the cutter of your rosary pliers to trim the end of the head-pin wire. Using the tip of your rosary plier, grasp the end of the wire stem. Roll the wire around the plier tip back toward the stem base to form a "c" shape.

Step 3: Hook the open end of the head-pin wire through the loop of the ear wire.

Step 4: Use the tip of your rosary pliers to continue to roll the wire stem to close the loop.

JUMP-RING DROP EARRINGS

• • • • • • • • • • •

Jump rings are not only a functional finding, but in this design they do double duty as an interesting chainmail style element. This project shows 4mm jump rings, but the finished piece will vary drastically depending on the size and quantity of rings you choose.

MATERIALS TO GATHER
- *Beads*
- *Head pins*
- *Jump rings*
- *Kidney ear wires*

TOOLS
- *Bead mat/rimmed tray for materials*
- *Rosary pliers*
- *Bent-nose pliers*

MAKE IT!

Step 1: Lay out your design, then place your beads in your desired order on the head pin. Holding the beads down to the bottom "head" of the pin in one hand, use the other hand to bend the end of the head-pin wire down just past a 90° angle.

Step 2: Leaving about ¼" of wire next to the bead, use the cutter of your rosary pliers to trim the end of the head-pin wire. Using your rosary pliers (to make a larger loop), grasp the end of the wire stem. Roll the wire around the plier tip back toward the stem base and close the loop.

Step 3: Using your bent-nose pliers, open up one jump ring and place two closed jump rings on. Then, close the opened jump ring.

(Continued on next page)

Step 4: Using your pliers, open up another jump ring and place it through the two closed jump rings, then close that ring. You are now forming a chain with a pattern of a single ring, a double ring, a single ring, etc. The more jump ring links you add, the longer the earrings will be.

Step 5: When your jump ring chain has reached its desired length, loop the top of the chain onto the kidney ear wire. Use the tip of your rosary pliers to pinch the neck of the kidney ear wire closed.

Pro Tip
When using jump rings that can open and close, make sure you are closing the rings tightly and evenly so that the split in the ring is nearly invisible.

Design Variations
- Vary the size of the jump rings to change the scale and style of the earrings.
- Add multiple bead drops to the bottom ring.
- Add bead drops onto each ring to create a cascading cluster effect.
- Use jump rings in different colors for a unique multicolor or ombré look.

FILIGREE BEADED EARRINGS

＊＊＊＊＊＊＊＊＊＊＊

Filigrees are a beautiful, intricate design element that takes a simple drop earring and elevates it to stylish new levels. These lovely findings come in all shapes, sizes, and finishes. Once you are comfortable with the design process, get bold and combine multiple filigrees with multiple beads to create some gorgeous statement pieces.

MATERIALS TO GATHER
- *Beads*
- *Head pins*
- *Filigrees*
- *Leverback earring wires*

TOOLS
- *Bead mat/rimmed tray for materials*
- *Rosary pliers*

MAKE IT!
Step 1: Lay out your design, then place your beads in your desired order on the head pin. Holding the bead(s) down to the bottom "head" of the pin in one hand, use the other hand to bend the end of the head-pin wire down just past a 90° angle.

Step 2: Leaving about ¼" of wire next to the bead, use the cutter of your rosary pliers to trim the end of the head-pin wire. Using the tip of your rosary plier, grasp the end of the wire stem. Roll the wire around the plier tip back toward the stem base to form a "c" shape.

Step 3: Hook the open end of the head-pin wire through the filigree. Then, use the tip of your rosary pliers to continue to roll the wire stem to close the loop.

(Continued on next page)

Step 4: Holding the leverback earring wire in one hand, use the top of your rosary pliers to open the front loop of the finding (using the same parallel twist motion as when you are opening a jump ring). Making sure the bead is centered at the bottom of the filigree, place the top opening of the filigree onto the open ear wire loop. Use your rosary plier tip to close the front loop of the ear wire.

Pro Tip
Filigrees come in all shapes and sizes. Make sure you choose one that has balanced open loops so that they hang straight.

Design Variations
- Combine multiple filigrees to create bold, dramatic statement earrings.
- Use craft paint or spray paint for a creative twist on an ornate filigree.
- Add multiple bead drops for a more boho-style design.
- Use eye pins to add beads to the earring design between the ear wire and the filigree.

BEADED STUD DROP EARRINGS

•–•–•–•–•–•–•–•–•

Studs are a classic earring style that can be simple and understated with a small bead, or big and bold with added elements such as filigrees, jump rings, and statement beads. This project shows you how the addition of bead caps and decorative stud findings can take a simple beaded drop and turn it into an elegant accessory worthy of a night on the town.

MATERIALS TO GATHER
- *Beads*
- *Head pins*
- *Post earring findings*

TOOLS
- *Bead mat/rimmed tray for materials*
- *Rosary pliers*

MAKE IT!

Step 1: Lay out your design, then place your beads in your desired order on the head pin. Holding the beads down to the bottom "head" of the pin in one hand, use the other hand to bend the end of the head-pin wire down just past a 90° angle.

Step 2: Leaving about ¼" of wire next to the bead, use the cutter of your rosary pliers to trim the end of the head-pin wire. Using the tip of your rosary plier, grasp the end of the wire stem. Roll the wire around the plier tip back toward the stem base to form a "c" shape.

Step 3: Hook the open end of the head-pin wire through the loop of the post earring finding. Then, use the tip of your rosary pliers to continue rolling the wire stem to close the loop.

Design Variations
- Make a statement earring by creating a long bead drop with multiple beads in the stack.
- Use jump rings to attach multiple beads for a more dramatic design.
- Use sterling silver or gold post findings with a single gemstone bead to create a high-quality pair of earrings without a tremendous cost.

BEADED HOOP EARRINGS

• • • • • • • • • •

Hoop earrings are a timeless classic, and the addition of beads makes them modern and fun. As you gain more experience and confidence in your jewelry-making skills, you may choose to create your own hoops using wire (materials like copper or steel work well for everyday wear, or you may prefer to work with a precious metal such as sterling silver or gold). Using premade hoop earring findings makes the design process fun and easy, leaving you free to be creative with your bead colors, patterns, and textures. As a bonus, hoop earring findings can double as wine glass charms (see page 96 for this project).

MATERIALS TO GATHER
- *Hoop earring findings*
- *Beads*

TOOLS
- *Bead mat/rimmed tray for materials*
- *Bent-nose pliers*

MAKE IT!

Step 1: Lay out your design, then open the hoop earring finding and slide on the beads in your desired pattern (you can either fill the entire hoop or leave some of the wire exposed as part of the design).

Step 2: Once you have finished adding beads, use your bent-nose pliers to grasp the end of the wire and bend it upward at a 90° angle. This is the part that goes through the ear and hooks into the back to close the earring and keeps the beads from sliding off of the hoop.

Step 3: Insert the end of the wire through the hole on the other side of the hoop to close the earring.

Design Variations
- Use bead drops spaced out with beads on the wire to create a more boho-style design.
- Use beads that are graduated in size, from the largest in the center of the hoop tapering out to the smallest at the end.
- Use multiple beads of the same size and shape in an ombré design.

STRUNG BEADED EARRINGS

Using beading string in this project allows you to create a natural teardrop-shaped earring. Smaller beads bend nicely with the wire, but if you prefer to use larger beads, make sure to use spacers so that the wire is not exposed in the finished earring.

MATERIALS TO GATHER
- Bead wire (preferably 49-strand)
- Beads
- Bead spacers (optional)
- Crimp tube
- Jump rings
- Crimp cover bead
- Leverback earring wires

TOOLS
- Bead mat/rimmed tray for materials
- Crimping pliers
- Cutters
- Bent-nose pliers

MAKE IT!

Step 1: Pull out 6" of wire from your roll. Lay out your design, then place the beads and bead spacers (if using) on the string, bringing the wire ends together periodically to see if your earrings are taking on the shape and size you desire.

Step 2: Once you have finished adding beads, place a crimp tube on the end of the wire. Loop the wire through a jump ring and back through the crimp tube, leaving about ¼" of wire beyond the tube.

Step 3: Using the dimpled part of your crimping pliers, create crimp in the tube. Using the open part of your crimping pliers, rotate the crimp ¼" and press again to close the crimp. Then, using the tip of your crimping pliers, press down on the closed crimp tube to flatten and further secure your crimp.

(Continued on next page)

Step 4: Using the open part of your crimping pliers, lightly grasp the crimp cover bead so that the opening is aligned with the opening of the pliers. Place the crimp cover bead over the crimp, then gently squeeze the pliers to close the bead around the crimp. You can either tuck the wire end into the end bead or if the hole is too small you can use your cutters to trim the wire to be flush with the crimp cover. Push the beads along the wire to be flush against the crimp bead. Leaving about 2" of wire, use your cutters to cut the wire off the spool. Repeat this step for the second end of the wire.

Step 5: Use the tip of your bent-nose pliers to open up the loop on the leverback earring wires, place the jump ring on the open loop, then close the loop tightly.

Pro Tip

Using a high-quality 49-strand wire will give you the most flexibility and strength. In a design like this, you want to make sure your wire is flexible enough to give you the ideal shape and movement.

Design Variations

- To alter the shape of the beaded teardrop, you can use a larger jump ring to connect. (A smaller jump ring will give you a more tapered top, while a larger jump ring will be more open.)
- Add a bead drop to the bottom of the jump ring *inside* the beaded teardrop for an interesting design element.
- Instead of a jump ring, attach the bead wire ends to a pretty filigree to create bold statement earrings.

CHAPTER 5
BRACELETS

Bracelets are a classic accessory for women and men of all ages. Beaded bracelets are eye-catching and fun to make, and there is a wide range of materials and techniques that you can use to create your pieces. When constructing your bracelets, take caution to choose materials that are sturdy, smooth, and comfortable. Bracelets are a "high touch" jewelry item, frequently coming into contact with hard surfaces such as tabletops and keyboards. You want to be sure your finished piece is wearable and strong.

STANDARD BRACELET LENGTHS

Wrist sizes are admittedly the toughest to gauge. Generally speaking, the sizes for women's bracelets are 6.5"–7.5" (with most standard women's bracelets being 7" long) and men's bracelets are 7.5"–9" (with most standard men's bracelets being 8" long). I personally prefer to create bracelets that have a little bit of room for adjustment when possible.

TECHNIQUES

The techniques you will use to complete the projects in this chapter include opening and closing jump rings, making loops, and stringing/crimping. Refer back to these techniques in Chapter 3 on page 16 as needed when you are working through these projects.

Pro Tip

Use more beads to make this piece longer and create a beautiful wrap-style bracelet.

Design Variations

- Memory wire bracelets are great for "bead soup" designs. Whip up a few of these when you have a nice collection of leftover beads from other projects.
- Get creative with the bead drops at the ends of the bracelets (think charms, multiple drops, and statement drops).
- Use a shorter length of memory wire to create a single strand cuff-style bracelet, or combine multiple single strands using a bead spacer to create a multi-strand cuff.

MEMORY WIRE BRACELET

• - • - • - • - • - • - • - •

Memory wire is a fun and forgiving way to create bracelets and, as a bonus, you don't even need to add a clasp! You can make the bracelet shorter if you only want it to wrap around the wrist once, or much longer if you want a bold statement piece. Larger beads will require a bit more wire to wrap around the wrist, while smaller beads will require less wire for the same length of wrap.

MATERIALS TO GATHER
- *Beads*
- *Memory wire (about 20" long)*
- *Head pins*
- *Jump rings*

TOOLS
- *Bead mat/rimmed tray for materials*
- *Rosary pliers or round-nose pliers*
- *Heavy-duty cutters*
- *Bent-nose pliers*

MAKE IT!

Step 1: Gather your materials and lay out your design on your bead mat. Leave a couple of beads to make decorative drops at the ends of the bracelet. String your beads onto the memory wire, periodically checking it on your wrist to make sure it's your desired length. When the bracelet has reached your desired length, use your rosary pliers or round-nose pliers to form a loop at the end of the wire.

Step 2: Push the beads onto the loop. Leaving about 1" of wire on the opposite end, use your heavy-duty cutters to cut the wire off the spool. Use your rosary/round-nose pliers to form a loop at this end of the wire.

Step 3: Using the head pins and remaining beads, create a bead drop for each end of the bracelet. Then, use your bent-nose and rosary pliers to attach a drop to the loop at each end of the bracelet with a jump ring.

STRETCH BEADED BRACELET

*Elastic cord bracelets are a fun way to make a quick and easy piece. Once you get the hang of the technique, you can create coordinating stacks of beaded bracelets that make a great statement accessory. Practice with inexpensive beads when you are first starting out with elastic, and make sure that you are working over a rimmed tray with a bead mat. While the creation process is simple, there's a definite method to learning how to properly stretch, hold, knot, and secure the elastic. Don't get frustrated if (okay, **when**) the elastic slips out of your hand and your beads go flying (hence the rimmed tray).*

MATERIALS TO GATHER
- *Elastic cord (0.7mm)*
- *Beads*
- *Superglue*

TOOLS
- *Bead mat/rimmed tray for materials*
- *Scissors*

MAKE IT!

Step 1: Gather your materials and lay out your design on your bead mat. Pull about 10" of elastic off the spool (leaving it attached) and pre-stretch the elastic. Add your beads onto the elastic cord.

Step 2: Leaving 2" at each end, use scissors to cut the cord off the spool while holding the ends to prevent the beads from slipping off. Tie off the ends using a surgeon's knot (see Chapter 3 on page 23 to review this technique). Dab a small dot of superglue on the knot and (if possible) slide it into an adjacent bead hole.

Pro Tip
When working with elastic, make sure to include at least one bead with a large hole to place next to the knot. This will allow you to easily slip the knot inside of the bead to hide!

Design Variations
- Attach the elastic ends to a decorative center finding such as a filigree or multi-strand focal to level up the design.
- Create a bracelet "stack" of multiple elastic bracelets, each one using a single type of bead, that can be worn together as a statement.
- If the closing knot is too large to tuck into a bead, try tying a bit of ribbon or lace over the top of it for an unexpected design twist.

Pro Tip

Adding a few extra jump rings or chain links at the end of the bracelet allows it to be adjusted a bit longer if necessary.

Design Variations

- Combine a shorter section of strung beads with longer sections of jump rings or decorative chain.
- Most bracelets will move around on the wearer's wrist but using a decorative clasp means that there's no "wrong" side of the piece.

STRUNG WIRE BRACELET

Beaded bracelets are fun and beautiful. When working with beading wire, make sure you choose a high-quality (49-strand is preferred), flexible wire so that your bracelet moves and lays beautifully. When working with wire that will be attached to a jump ring, I prefer to use a wire protector. This is a small finding that protects the wire from scraping up against sharp edges, wearing down over time. A wire protector is a nice finishing touch, but it's not an essential element to the completed piece.

MATERIALS TO GATHER
- Bead wire
- Beads
- Crimp tubes
- Wire protector (optional)
- Jump rings
- Crimp cover bead
- Clasp

TOOLS
- Bead mat/rimmed tray for materials
- Crimping pliers
- Cutters/scissors

MAKE IT!
Step 1: Gather your materials and lay out your design on your bead mat. Leaving the bead wire attached to the spool, pull out about 8" of wire.

Step 2: Following your pattern, add your beads to the wire. After the beads have all been added, place a crimp tube and wire protector (if using) on the wire.

Step 3: Loop the wire through a jump ring and back through the bead crimp, leaving about ¼" of wire past the end of the crimp tube. Using your crimping pliers, crimp the tube closed. Using the tip of your crimping pliers, cover the crimp with the crimp cover bead.

Step 4: Move the beads to be flush against the crimp cover bead, tucking the tail of the wire into the end bead. Trim with your cutters or scissors if necessary. Leaving about 2" of wire, trim the wire off the spool. Repeat steps to loop the remaining wire through the clasp.

MULTI-STRAND STRUNG WIRE BRACELET

This project challenges you to create a beaded bracelet with multiple strands of beads. Having a bead board that is designed for bracelets makes these projects much easier to lay out and complete. I suggest starting out with two strands to practice. Once you get the hang of it, you can go as big and bold as your heart desires!

MATERIALS TO GATHER
- 2-hole spacer bars
- Bead wire
- Beads
- Crimp tubes
- 2 multi-strand ends
- Crimp cover beads
- Jump rings
- Clasp

TOOLS
- Bead mat/rimmed tray for materials
- Crimping pliers
- Cutters/scissors

MAKE IT!

Step 1: Gather your materials and lay out your design on your bead mat. You will be laying out two strands of beaded designs; both strands should be the same length. Place the spacer bars approximately every 2"–3", making sure to have the same amount of space in between. If the beads are the same size, measure by using the same number of beads. If the beads are varying sizes, measure by using the same length of the layout.

Step 2: Leaving the bead wire attached to the spool, pull out about 8" of wire. Following your pattern, add your beads to the wire.

Step 3: After the beads have all been added, place a crimp tube on the wire. Loop the wire through the bottom hole of one multi-strand end and back through the bead crimp, leaving about ¼" of wire past the end of the crimp tube. Using your crimping pliers, crimp the tube closed and secure. Using the tip of your crimping pliers, cover the crimp with the crimp cover bead.

(Continued on next page)

Step 4: Move the beads to be flush against the crimp cover bead, tucking the tail of the wire into the end bead (trim with your cutters or scissors if necessary). Leaving about 2" of wire, trim the wire off the spool. Repeat steps to attach the wire to the remaining multi-strand end.

Step 5: With the second strand, repeat steps to run the wire through the top hole of the spacer bar and loop the wire through the top hole of the multi-strand end.

Step 6: Using a jump ring, attach the clasp to one end of the bracelet. Add a jump ring or links of chain on the other end of the bracelet to make it adjustable for the wearer.

Pro Tip

Leave a little bit of room for flexibility in the wire when you are attaching it to the multi-strand end. You want the beads to be able to move a tiny bit so that they lay nicely and the bracelet closes easily.

Design Variations

- Choose one consistent element to carry throughout your bead design: the same color, the same size, the same pattern, etc.
- If you want to use larger beads for your bracelet, you can use a spacer bar that is designed for four strands but only use two strands to accommodate the bead size.

FILIGREE FINDING BRACELET

· · · · · · · · · · · ·

Filigrees come in a wide variety of shapes, sizes, and designs. These can really add a unique element to your design: They also can be a fun connector piece for multi-strand bracelets. When choosing a filigree, make sure it has evenly spaced openings for you to run your bead wire through if you want to create a symmetrical design.

For this design, I am placing a single filigree in the center of the bracelet, however, you can be creative with either multiple filigrees or multiple strands of beads.

MATERIALS TO GATHER

- *Bead wire*
- *Beads*
- *Crimp tubes*
- *Filigree findings*
- *Crimp cover bead*
- *Jump rings*
- *Clasp*

TOOLS

- *Bead mat/rimmed tray for materials*
- *Crimping pliers*
- *Cutters/scissors*

MAKE IT!

Step 1: Gather your materials and lay out your design on your bead mat. Leaving the bead wire attached to the spool, pull out about 6" of wire.

Step 2: Following your pattern, add your beads to the wire. Once all the beads have been added, place a crimp tube on the end of the wire.

Step 3: Loop the wire through one filigree finding and back through the bead crimp, leaving about ¼" of wire past the end of the crimp tube.

(Continued on next page)

Step 4: Using your crimping pliers, crimp the tube closed. Using the tip of your crimping pliers, cover the crimp with the crimp cover bead. Move the beads to be flush against the crimp cover bead, tucking the tail of the wire into the end bead. Trim with your cutters or scissors if necessary. Leaving about 2" of wire, trim the wire off the spool.

Step 5: Repeat steps and loop the wire through a jump ring. Then, repeat steps for the other side of the bracelet and loop the wire through the clasp.

Pro Tip

Adding a few extra jump rings or chain links at the end of the bracelet allows it to be adjusted a bit longer if necessary.

Design Variations

- Multiple strands of beautiful beads are the perfect pair to a filigree focal piece.
- Connect multiple filigrees with beaded eye pins.
- Use the techniques from the Charm Bracelet on page 59 to add beaded chain on either side of the filigree focal.

CHARM BRACELET

· · · · · · · · · · ·

Charm-style bracelets are beautiful statement pieces that can be designed by color, shape, size, or as a place to gather sentimental charms and pieces. The design possibilities are endless!

MATERIALS TO GATHER
- Beads
- Head pins
- Link chain (bracelet size)
- Jump rings
- Charms (optional)
- Lobster-claw clasp

TOOLS
- Bead mat/rimmed tray for materials
- Bent-nose pliers
- Rosary pliers

MAKE IT!

Step 1: Gather your materials and lay out your design on your bead mat. Place your bead(s) on a head pin and make a loop, creating bead drops. Repeat this for all your beads, laying them back down on your mat in the order that you'd like to add them to the bracelet.

Step 2: Lay out the link chain so that the links are smooth and evenly spaced (careful not to twist the chain).

Step 3: Starting at one end, use your bent-nose and rosary pliers to attach a bead drop to the bottom side of one chain link with a jump ring. Skip one link, then attach the next bead drop to the top side of the next link. Continue this pattern until you reach the end of the chain.

(Continued on next page)

Step 4: Fill in additional bead drops or charms (if using) on the top side of the empty chain links (the ones you skipped in Step 3), making sure to attach the jump ring to the same edge of the link all the way down the chain. Using your bent-nose and rosary pliers to attach the lobster-claw clasp to one end of the chain with a jump ring.

Pro Tip
If you have a "third hand" tool to hold each end of the chain, you will be able to easily add the beads and charms in a balanced pattern.

Design Variations
- Create a "full" look for your bracelet by adding multiple bead drops to each link.
- Vary the size of the beads for a curated, styled look.
- Use decorative head pins to change up the look of the bead drops.

Chapter 6
NECKLACES

· · · · · · · · · · · ·

Now that you've had the chance to practice some of the basic beading techniques on smaller projects, you are ready to dive into necklaces! Necklaces are a virtual staple in every woman's accessory wardrobe. Creating them with beads gives you the flexibility to really let your creativity shine!

STANDARD NECKLACE LENGTHS

The length of the piece you create can dramatically change the look and feel of it, from a casual long layering piece to a stunning formal choker. Different people prefer different lengths of necklace, and each one "wears" differently from person to person depending on neck size, height, and body type. Here are some of the most common necklace lengths and their descriptions:

Collar length (12"–14"): This is a very short and snug fit, typically seen in vintage necklaces or ribbon-style choker necklaces.

Choker length (14"–16"): This is slightly longer than collar length, with the necklace resting snugly at the base of the throat.

Princess length (18"): This length sits at or near the collarbone.

Matinee length (20"–24"): This length sits between the collarbone and the bustline and is one of the most popular lengths for beaded necklaces.

Opera length (28"–36"): This length sits at the bustline or a few inches below, depending on the wearer's body type.

Rope length (36"–42"): This length worn as-is will hang below the bust and doubled or wrapped will sit at or above bust level.

TECHNIQUES

The techniques you will use to complete the projects in this chapter include opening and closing jump rings, making loops, and stringing. Refer back to these techniques in Chapter 3 on page 16 as needed when you are working through these projects. The projects in this book are all shown at either princess or matinee length, but the techniques remain the same regardless of the length you choose. Make sure you take into account the weight of the finished piece, the occasion you are designing for, and the cost of materials when deciding upon a length. Some of the projects shown include optional "extra" findings such as bead spacers, wire protectors, crimp tube covers, and wire wrapping beads (see more findings in Chapter 1 on pages 5–9).

Design Variations

- Let this single strand necklace make a statement by designing a bold pattern with your beads. Color blocking and graduated bead sizes are two easy ways to level up the design.
- Add a bail to the center of the design that will allow you to attach a pendant.
- Dramatize one design element, such as the length, to add instant interest to an otherwise simple piece.

SINGLE STRAND BEADED NECKLACE

You can't go wrong with a single strand necklace, right? Strings of beads are a classic look at any length and allow the beauty of the beads themselves to take center stage as the main design element. When choosing your beads for this simple piece, balance is key. If the beads are all the same size, you can add an interesting element by color blocking beads or creating a mix of different coordinating colors and stones. If the beads are different sizes, make sure you lay out the necklace so that the "weight" or largest beads are in the center, tapering out to the smaller beads on the ends.

MATERIALS TO GATHER
- *Bead wire*
- *Beads*
- *Crimp tubes*
- *Jump rings*
- *Crimp cover bead*
- *Clasp*

TOOLS
- *Bead mat/rimmed tray for materials*
- *Crimping pliers*
- *Cutters/scissors*

MAKE IT!
Step 1: Gather your materials and lay out your design on your bead mat. Leaving the bead wire attached to the spool, pull out about 20" of wire.

Step 2: Following your pattern, add your beads to the wire. After the beads have all been added, place a crimp tube on the wire.

Step 3: Loop the wire through a jump ring and back through the bead crimp, leaving about ¼" of wire past the end of the crimp tube. Using your crimping pliers, crimp the tube closed. Using the tip of your crimping pliers, cover the crimp with the crimp cover bead.

Step 4: Move the beads to be flush against the crimp cover bead, tucking the tail of the wire into the end bead. Trim with your cutters/scissors if necessary. Leaving about 2" of wire, trim the wire off the spool.

Step 5: Repeat steps to loop the remaining wire through the clasp.

BEADED PENDANT NECKLACE

• • • • • • • • • • •

Pendant style necklaces are a great way to create a simple or bold statement. For this design, I use a closed ring as the center focal with a bead pendant attached. Once you are comfortable with the technique, you can get creative with your pendant options. Filigrees, multiple bead drops, or even a toggle clasp as the focal with a bead or charm pendant can be interesting variations on this design.

MATERIALS TO GATHER

- *Bead wire*
- *Beads*
- *Closed ring finding*
- *Crimp tubes*
- *Crimp cover bead*
- *Bead for pendant*
- *Bead caps*
- *Head pins (long enough to go through the pendant bead)*
- *Jump rings*
- *Clasp*

TOOLS

- *Bead mat/rimmed tray for materials*
- *Crimping pliers*
- *Cutters/scissors*
- *Bent-nose pliers*
- *Rosary pliers*

MAKE IT!

Step 1: Gather your materials and lay out your design on your bead mat. Leaving the bead wire attached to the spool, pull out about 10" of bead wire. Following your pattern, add your beads and bead spacers to the wire.

Step 2: Loop the wire through the closed ring finding and back through the bead crimp, leaving about ¼" of wire past the end of the crimp tube. Using your crimping pliers, crimp the tube closed. Using the tip of your crimping pliers, cover the crimp with the crimp cover bead.

Step 3: Move the beads to be flush against the crimp cover bead, tucking the tail of the wire into the end bead. Trim with your cutters/scissors if necessary. Leaving about 2" of wire, trim the wire off the spool.

(Continued on next page)

Step 4: Repeat steps to loop the wire through a jump ring. Then, repeat steps for the other side of the necklace and loop the wire through another jump ring. Use your bent-nose and rosary pliers to attach the clasp to one end of the necklace with a jump ring.

Make the Pendant

Step 1: Stack the bead cap and bead onto a head pin. Holding the beads down to the bottom "head" of the pin in one hand, use the other hand to bend the end of the head-pin wire down just past a 90° angle.

Step 2: Leaving about ½" of wire next to the bead, use the cutter of your rosary pliers to trim the end of the head-pin wire. Using the tip of your rosary pliers, grasp the end of the wire stem. Roll the wire around the plier tip back toward the stem base to form a "c" shape.

Step 3: Hook the open end of the head-pin wire through the closed ring at the center of the necklace. Use the tip of your rosary pliers to continue to roll the wire stem to close the loop.

Make the Extender Bead Dangle

Step 1: Place a bead on a head pin. I prefer to use a bead that matches the beads that make up the body of the necklace.

Step 2: Repeat steps from the pendant instructions above and hook the open end of the head-pin wire through the last jump ring or link at the end of the necklace extension.

BEADED CHAIN NECKLACE

· • · • · • · • · • · ·

In this project, the chain takes center stage to create a lightweight necklace. I love experimenting with different kinds of chains. As you get more comfortable with this technique, you can design with multiple strands of chains or even combine different chains to create a unique texture. This is also a great project design to feature a small number of high-quality beads, such as gemstones or genuine pearls, without breaking the bank.

MATERIALS TO GATHER

- Bead wire
- Beads
- Crimp tubes
- 2 (7") chains
- Crimp cover bead
- Jump rings
- Clasp
- Head pin

TOOLS

- Bead mat/rimmed tray for materials
- Crimping pliers
- Cutters/scissors
- Bent-nose pliers
- Rosary pliers

MAKE IT!

Step 1: Gather your materials and lay out your design on your bead mat. Leaving the bead wire attached to the spool, pull out about 8" of wire. Following your pattern, add your beads to the wire.

Step 2: After the beads have all been added, place a crimp tube on the wire. Loop the wire through the end of one of the chains and back through the bead crimp, leaving about ¼" of wire past the end of the crimp tube. Using your crimping pliers, crimp the tube closed. Using the tip of your crimping pliers, cover the crimp with the crimp cover bead.

Step 3: Move the beads to be flush against the crimp cover bead, tucking the tail of the wire into the end bead. Trim with your cutters/scissors if necessary. Leaving about 2" of wire, trim the wire off the spool.

(Continued on next page)

Step 4: Repeat steps and loop the remaining wire through the end of the other piece of chain.

Step 5: Use your bent-nose and rosary pliers to attach a clasp to one side of the chain end and the extender bead dangle to the other side of the chain using jump rings.

Make the Extender Bead Dangle

Step 1: Stack a bead (I suggest using the same bead type as the focal strand) on to a head pin. Holding the bead down to the bottom "head" of the pin in one hand, use the other hand to bend the end of the head-pin wire down just past a 90° angle.

Step 2: Leaving about ½" of wire next to the bead, use the cutter of your rosary pliers to trim the end of the head-pin wire. Using the tip of your rosary pliers, grasp the end of the wire stem. Roll the wire around the plier tip back toward the stem base to form a "c" shape.

Step 3: Hook the open end of the head-pin wire through the closed ring at the center of the necklace. Use the tip of your rosary pliers to continue to roll the wire stem to close the loop.

Pro Tip
Make sure the chain you use is in balance with the beads you choose. Larger open links pair well with larger beads, while smaller links pair nicely with small beads or pearls.

Design Variations
- Combine 2–3 strands of chain in varying styles or finishes to create a unique, multi-strand look. Connect the beaded center to a large jump ring or solid ring that will connect the multiple chains to the beads.
- Use multiple small strands of beads in varying lengths to create a graduated, multi-strand bead focal.
- Use jump rings to add bead drops along the chain links to create a fun and funky statement piece.

ROSARY-STYLE BEADED NECKLACE

This is one of my favorite styles of necklace to make because there's so much room for flexibility in both design and length, and it's quick and easy to switch up components if you decide to change the look of the piece.

MATERIALS TO GATHER
- Beads
- Eye-pin wires
- Charms/beads (for the focal bead cluster)
- Head pins
- Jump rings
- Toggle-style clasp
- 1 (3–4 open-link) chain or 2–3 jump rings linked together

TOOLS
- Bead mat/rimmed tray for materials
- Rosary pliers
- Cutters/scissors
- Bent-nose pliers

MAKE IT!

Step 1: Gather your materials and lay out your design on your bead mat. Starting at one end of your design, place the bead (or bead stack) onto an eye-pin wire.

Step 2: Holding the beads down to the bottom "eye" of the pin in one hand, use the other hand to bend the end of the eye-pin wire down just past a 90° angle. Leaving about ½" of wire next to the bead, use the cutter of your rosary pliers to trim the end of the eye-pin wire. Using the tip of your rosary pliers, grasp the end of the wire stem. Roll the wire around the plier tip back toward the stem base to form a closed loop. Add a bead (or bead stack) to another empty eye pin, then repeat these steps, this time leaving the loop open in a "c" shape.

Step 3: Hook the open end of the eye-pin wire through the closed loop of the first bead stack. Use the tip of your rosary pliers to continue to roll the wire stem to close the loop. Repeat these steps until you have reached your desired length to create a beaded rosary style chain.

(Continued on next page)

Step 4: With your bent-nose and rosary pliers, attach the open piece of the toggle clasp to one end of the necklace using a jump ring. Using 2–3 jump rings (this makes it easier to slide the toggle through the clasp opening), attach the bar piece of the toggle clasp to the other end of the necklace.

Make the Bead Cluster

Step 1: Open the end link of your open-link chain or jump rings linked together and attach it to the open piece of the toggle clasp.

Step 2: Using head pins, wire wrap any of the beads that are going to be added to this chain.

Step 3: Using jump rings, attach the wire-wrapped beads and charms to the chain.

MULTI-STRAND BEADED NECKLACE

A multi-strand beaded necklace is a beautiful way to create a statement piece that shows off some gorgeous beads. To make designing this project easier, I suggest using a bead board that allows you to lay out multiple strands of a necklace. You want to use the channels that are adjacent to each other to make sure that the length of each strand is appropriate for the finished piece to lay nicely.

MATERIALS TO GATHER

- Bead wire
- Beads/bead spacers (for body of necklace and extender bead dangle)
- Crimp tubes
- Crimp cover bead
- Jump rings
- 2 multi-strand ends
- Clasp
- Head pin

TOOLS

- Bead mat/rimmed tray for materials
- Crimping pliers
- Cutters/scissors
- Bent-nose pliers
- Rosary pliers

MAKE IT!

Step 1: Gather your materials and lay out your design on your bead mat. Lay out two strands of beaded designs. One strand should be slightly shorter than the other.

Step 2: Leaving the bead wire attached to the spool, pull out about 16"–18" of wire. Following your pattern for the shorter strand, add your beads to the wire.

Step 3: After the beads have all been added, place a crimp tube on the wire. Loop the wire through the top hole of the multi-strand end and back through the bead crimp, leaving about ¼" of wire past the end of the crimp tube. Using your crimping pliers, crimp the tube closed. Using the tip of your crimping pliers, cover the crimp with the crimp cover bead.

(Continued on next page)

Step 4: Move the beads to be flush against the crimp cover bead, tucking the tail of the wire into the end bead. Trim with your cutters/scissors if necessary.

Step 5: Leaving about 2" of wire, trim the wire off the spool. Repeat steps with the other end of the strand and attach it to the top hole of the other multi-strand end. Repeat steps for the longer strand, attaching it to the bottom hole of each multi-strand end.

Step 6: Use your bent-nose and rosary pliers to attach one of the multi-strand ends to a clasp using a jump ring. Hooking together 3 to 4 jump rings to form a chain, attach the jump-ring chain to the other multi-strand end. Using a head pin and a bead, create a bead dangle for the end of the jump-ring chain and attach.

Design Variations

- Use 3-,4-, or even 5-strand connectors to create bold statement necklaces.
- Turn the necklace around to make the connector ends the focal. Connect them to a toggle clasp and add a bead cluster like the one in the Rosary-Style Beaded Necklace on page 71.
- Add bead drops and earring wires to multi-strand ends to make beautiful chandelier-style earrings.

Pro Tip

For a variation on this design, shorten the beaded portion and use an interesting chain (similar to the Beaded Chain Necklace on page 67) to complete the piece.

MEMORY WIRE BEADED NECKLACE

Memory wire necklaces work best at choker-length due to the rigid nature of the material, which also makes them the perfect candidate to use some larger beads. I recommend using more lightweight beads if you aren't going to add a clasp on the ends.

MATERIALS TO GATHER
- *Beads*
- *Memory wire (necklace size)*
- *Head pins*
- *Jump rings*

TOOLS
- *Bead mat/rimmed tray for materials*
- *Bent-nose pliers*
- *Heavy-duty cutters*
- *Rosary pliers*

MAKE IT!
Step 1: Gather your materials and lay out your design on your bead mat. Leave a few beads to make decorative drops at the ends of the necklace. String your beads onto the memory wire, periodically checking it on your neck to make sure it's your desired length. When the necklace has reached your desired length, use your bent-nose pliers to form a loop at the end of the wire.

Step 2: Push the beads to the loop. Leaving about 1" of wire, use your heavy-duty cutters to cut the wire off the spool. Use your bent-nose pliers to form a loop at this end of the wire. Note: Be careful to hold on tightly as you cut the wire. This will act like a spring and could send beads sailing all over the room when the wire bounces after being cut!

Step 3 (Optional): Using the head pins and remaining beads, create a bead drop for each end of the necklace and use jump rings to attach.

Design Variations
- Add bead drops in between the beads for more fun and movement.
- Use spacer bars to connect and create a multi-strand choker necklace.
- To create a "floating" bead look, place a covered bead crimp closely on either side of a bead (to hold it in place) and space these out along the wire.

KNOTTED BEADED NECKLACE

· - · - · - · - · - · - ·

Knotted strands aren't just for pearls (although you surely can't go wrong with them). This beading technique is more advanced in that it takes a bit longer to learn how to get the knot close enough (but not too tight) to the bead. Once you get the hang of knotting, you will find yourself returning to this project time and time again. Refer to Chapter 3 on page 22 to see step-by-step instructions for knotting beads.

MATERIALS TO GATHER
- *Beading cord of choice*
- *Clamshell knot cover connector*
- *Superglue*
- *Beads*
- *Clasp*
- *Jump rings*

TOOLS
- *Bead mat/rimmed tray for materials*
- *Beading needle*
- *Bent-nose pliers*
- *Rosary pliers/round-nose pliers*
- *Awl*
- *Scissors*

MAKE IT!
Step 1: Cut a length of beading cord at least 3 to 4 times the desired length of the project. At one end of the cord, tie a tight knot about ½"–1" away from the end. (If your cord is thin, you may choose to tie multiple knots.) Slide the other end of the cord through the beading needle.

Step 2: Slide the needle through the clamshell knot cover connector so that the knot rests inside the cup. Optional: Add a dot of superglue on the knot here for extra security.

Step 3: Using the flat edge of your bent-nose pliers, squeeze the clamshell closed. Then, use the tip of your rosary pliers (or round-nose pliers) to close the loop on the end of the connector.

(Continued on next page)

Step 4: Slide a bead onto the cord. Loosely tie a knot in the cord close to the bead, then use the awl to slide the knot down so that it's right next to the bead. Pull out the awl and tighten the knot. Repeat until the necklace is as long as you'd like it to be.

Step 5: When you've added the last bead, slide the needle through the bottom site of a second clamshell knot cover. Tie a knot, using your awl to keep the knot and knot cover close to the end bead.

Step 6: Close the clamshell, trim any excess cord, and attach a clasp and jump ring at the ends of the necklace.

Pro Tip
Periodically test the flexibility of the necklace as you are working. If the knots are too tight against the beads, the necklace will not lay nicely. You want to find the "sweet spot" where the knot will rest comfortably next to the bead with just a hint of wiggle room.

Design Variations
- Choose a bold-colored bead cord that contrasts or complements the beads.
- Use multiple strands of thin cord to create a unique ombré or rainbow look.
- Connect a strand of knotted beads to a bold chain.

CHAPTER 7
RINGS

· · · · · · · · · · ·

Everyone loves a good statement ring. Whether you are creating a wire-wrapped beauty or using a pre-created ring finding, these projects will quickly have you hooked.

STANDARD RING SIZES

Ring sizes vary widely, but there are a few "standards" that will help you decide where to start. With traditional ring sizing, each size and half-size is measured in 0.4mm diameter increments (starting at 14mm) as follows:

Size 3: 14mm

Size 3.5: 14.4mm

Size 4: 14.8mm

Size 4.5: 15.2mm

Size 5: 15.6 mm

Size 5.5: 16mm

Size 6: 16.4mm

Size 6.5: 16.8mm

Size 7: 17.2mm

Size 7.5: 17.6mm

Size 8: 18mm

Size 8.5: 18.4mm

Size 9: 18.8mm

Size 9.5: 19.2mm

Size 10: 19.6mm

Size 10.5: 20mm

Size 11: 20.4mm

Size 11.5: 20.8mm

Size 12: 21.2mm

Standard ring finger sizes for women are usually 6–8, while standard ring finger sizes for men are usually 10–12. If you are making a ring for yourself or for someone you know, the best way to figure out ring size is to use a ring sizing tool and a ring mandrel when making.

RING STYLES

There are two different types of ring projects that I will cover in this book: One uses wire wrapping and the other uses prefabricated ring findings. The wire-wrapped rings are created to size and do not have much room for size adjustment once they have been made. This method takes some time to perfect, so my suggestion is to practice with a higher-gauge (thinner) wire until you get more comfortable with the technique. Lower gauge (thicker) wires are a little bit more difficult to work with as they are significantly less flexible. Prefabricated ring findings come in both fixed and adjustable sizes, giving you some (literal) wiggle room to work with if you are creating rings and you aren't sure of the wearer's size. We will be using an elastic adjustable ring setting for our projects, but I urge you to explore all of the different types of prefabricated ring settings once you are comfortable with these techniques.

Design Variations

- Experiment with different colored copper wire for a unique design element.
- Replace one large singular focal with 2 to 3 smaller beads, using the same method to center and wire wrap around them.
- Select a shaped bead, such as a heart or triangle, for the focal.

WIRE-WRAPPED SINGLE BEAD RING

This ring-making project is a great one to start with. I suggest selecting one really beautiful statement bead (perhaps even a gemstone bead if you have one), since this one bead will take center stage in the design. When you are choosing what kind of bead you want to use, remember that the larger the bead, the higher it will sit on your hand. I do suggest practicing this technique with a higher gauge wire until you are comfortable, then moving into a lower gauge wire for a sturdier end result.

MATERIALS TO GATHER
- 1 (6–10mm) statement bead
- 1 (20–22-gauge) wire (the higher the gauge, the thinner the wire), approximately 22" long

TOOLS
- Bead mat/rimmed tray for materials
- Ring mandrel
- Bent-nose or chain-nose pliers
- Cutters
- Rubber mallet

MAKE IT!

Step 1: Place your bead on the wire, moving it to the center. Line the centered bead up on your mandrel in a position that's one full size larger than your desired end ring size. Position this two sizes larger if you are using a large focal bead.

Step 2: Wrap one side of the wire around the mandrel as many times as you'd like (3 to 4 times around will give you 3 to 4 wires in the ring band). Gently squeeze the wire bands down to be near the bead.

(Continued on next page)

Step 3: Grasping one end of the wire to keep it taut, grasp the other end and start to wrap it around the center bead (each wrap of the wire will sit underneath the one before it, gently pushing the center bead upward). Keep the wires taut and alternate wrapping around the center bead until you have 3 to 4 full wraps.

Step 4: Take the ring off the mandrel and move the wire ends so that you have one end going up and one end going down. With the end of the wire that's pointing up, wrap the end of the wire around the ring band wires, being careful to keep the coil close. Use your pliers to pull the wire taut. Wrap the wire around 3 to 4 times (the more wraps you make, the smaller the ring will be). Turn the ring over and repeat this step on the other side, making sure to wrap the wire the same number of times on the other side.

Step 5: Place your ring back on the mandrel, pulling it down so that the wires of the band straighten out neatly. Trim the excess wire, tucking the end into the coil or the band. After trimming and tucking the wire, place the ring on the mandrel one more time and tap with the rubber mallet to make sure the shape is set.

WIRE-WRAPPED MULTI-BEAD RING

· · · · · · · · · · ·

Although it may look more complicated, you might find this multi-bead ring a little bit easier to create than the previous wire-wrapped single bead ring. When selecting your materials, remember that the bead size will have an effect on how much wire you use and how high the final ring will sit on your hand. I suggest selecting 4 to 6 beads, no larger than 4mm each. Round, oval, cube, or rectangular beads tend to work best here.

MATERIALS TO GATHER
- 1 (20–22-gauge) wire (the higher the gauge, the thinner the wire), approximately 6" long
- 6 (2–4mm) beads

TOOLS
- Bead mat/rimmed tray for materials
- Ring mandrel
- Cutters
- Bent-nose or chain-nose pliers
- Rubber mallet

MAKE IT!

Step 1: Line the center of the wire up on your mandrel in a position that's a half-size larger than your desired end ring size (i.e., if you want the ring to be a size 7, position the center of the wire on the size 7.5 line). Wrap the ends of the wire around the mandrel so that each end of the wire is pointing out.

Step 2: Take the ring off the mandrel. Add 3 beads onto one end of the wire and 3 beads onto the other end, moving them into the middle to line up next to each other.

(Continued on next page)

Step 3: Bend the end of the wire of the bottom row at a 90° angle toward the top row of beads and bend the end of the wire of the bottom row at a 90° angle toward the bottom row of beads. Wrap one end of the wire around the band 2 to 3 times, making sure to keep the wire snug against the bead rows to create a coil. Repeat this with the other end of the wire.

Step 4: Using your cutters, trim the end of the wire. Use your bent-nose or chain-nose pliers to tuck in the end of the wire, then place the ring back on the mandrel, using the rubber mallet if needed to shape it.

Pro Tip

If you are choosing multiple beads, make sure they are the same or similar in size so that the wire wrapping and ring size are evenly balanced.

Design Variations

- Create a "mother's ring" by selecting beads to represent birthstones of children and other family members.
- Design a pattern of shaped beads to sit snugly together by alternating round and cube beads, oval and rectangular beads, etc.
- Use large-holed beads and two slightly higher gauge wires for a funky spin on this traditional design.

BEADED STATEMENT RING

· · · · · · · · · · ·

Working with prefabricated ring findings means that you get to put all your creative efforts into selecting and laying out your bead design. Choosing a finding that is adjustable gives you more flexibility in how you (or your giftee) will wear the ring.

MATERIALS TO GATHER
- 2–4mm beads
- Adjustable prefabricated ring finding
- 6–9 head pins

TOOLS
- Bead mat/rimmed tray for materials
- Bent-nose or chain-nose pliers
- Cutters
- Rosary pliers

MAKE IT!
Step 1: Lay out your bead design, stacking the bead(s) onto the head pins. If you are using multiple beads, make sure the bead you want to show at the top of the ring is at the bottom of the bead stack (against the "head" of the pin).

Step 2: Starting at one corner of the ring finding, insert the end of one of the head pins into the hole from the top down. With your bent-nose or chain-nose pliers, bend the wire at a 90° angle (or as close to 90° as you can get) against the bottom of the setting, then trim the end of the wire to leave approximately ¼" of wire past the bend.

Step 3: Using the tip of your rosary pliers, roll the end of the wire around to form a loop. This loop should be snug against the underside of the ring finding, leaving just a little bit of room for the head pin and beads to move. Repeat steps for the remaining 8 bead stacks.

Chapter 8
BONUS PROJECTS

The most wonderful thing about making beaded jewelry is . . . beads! There's an infinite supply of them in every shape, color, size, material, and finish you could possibly imagine, and once you get hooked on this hobby, you're going to want to add some of each to your collection. So, now that you've started creating beautiful, wearable pieces of art, you are probably finding yourself with an ever-growing collection of "leftover beads." I'm pretty confident that crafters everywhere have at least one little container full of beads that are just waiting for the perfect project. In this chapter, I'm going to show you six of my favorite non-jewelry projects that are the perfect way to use up those miscellaneous beads.

ZIPPER PULLS

· · · · · · · · · · · · ·

A zipper pull is a really fun way to use up extra beads and add some unexpected flair to your wardrobe. Choose your material size relative to what you will be putting the zipper pull on. For a small zipper you'll use a smaller claw and bead, and for a larger zipper you'll use larger materials.

MATERIALS TO GATHER
- *Beads*
- *Head pins*
- *Swivel clasp or large lobster-claw clasp*

TOOLS
- *Bead mat/rimmed tray for materials*
- *Cutters*
- *Rosary pliers*

MAKE IT!

Step 1: Lay out your bead design, stacking the bead(s) onto the headpins. If you are using multiple beads, use the largest/heaviest bead at the bottom. Be sure to leave at least ¾" of wire at the end of the pin.

Step 2: Bend the wire at a 90° angle against the bottom of the setting, leaving approximately ½" of wire past the bend. With your cutters, trim off the excess wire.

Step 3: Using the wide base of your rosary pliers, roll the wire around the pliers to form a large "c" shape (do not close the loop). Place the wire end through the bottom end of the clasp. Use the tip of your rosary pliers to finish closing the loop.

> ### PRO TIP
> If you are wanting to use multiple pins of beads to create a "jumble" for the pull, you can add in a closed ring or jump ring to attach the beads to the clasp. This will ensure that the pull hangs nicely and has some movement.

WINE GLASS CHARMS

· · · · · · · · · · · ·

Wine glass charms are an unexpectedly useful accessory to have on hand. These make great hostess gifts as well as functional party accessories. To make this project even easier, you can use premade hoop earring findings instead of creating your own wire loops from scratch.

MATERIALS TO GATHER
- Beads
- Head pins
- Hoop earring findings
- Charms (optional)

TOOLS
- Bead mat/rimmed tray for materials
- Rosary pliers
- Bent-nose pliers

MAKE IT!
Step 1: Lay out your bead design and stack your beads on the head pin. Holding the beads down to the bottom "head" of the pin in one hand, use the other hand to bend the end of the head-pin wire down just past a 90° angle.

Step 2: Using your rosary pliers, grasp the wire stem about ¼" from the bend. Roll the wire completely around the middle of the pliers, bringing the end of the wire back to its initial position.

Step 3: Holding the loop in place on the rosary pliers, use your fingers to wrap the end of the wire around the base of the loop. With the tip of your bent-nose pliers, tuck the end of the wire into place so that there are no points sticking out.

Step 4: Slide your beaded head pin onto the hoop earring finding. If you are adding multiple beaded head pins or charms (if using), continue to add those until they are all on the finding.

Step 5: Holding the hoop earring finding in one hand, use the tip of your bent-nose pliers to bend the end of the wire up to a 90° angle. Insert the end of the wire through the hole on the other side of the hoop to close the earring.

Pro Tip

If you are using prefabricated charms, use a jump ring to attach the charm to the hoop finding to allow it to lay properly. String small beads directly onto the wire with a charm in the middle as an alternative design.

KEYCHAINS

• • • • • • • • • • • •

Keychains are another great way to use some of your leftover beads. You will want to choose beads and materials that are sturdy and strong enough to withstand being bumped around against keys and the inside of bags. I recommend using the wire-wrapping technique for each bead for extra security.

MATERIALS TO GATHER
- Beads
- Head pins
- Solid ring
- Jump rings
- Split-ring keychain

TOOLS
- Bead mat/rimmed tray for materials
- Rosary pliers
- Bent-nose or chain-nose pliers

MAKE IT!

Step 1: Lay out your bead design, stacking the bead(s) onto the head pins. If you are using multiple beads on a pin, use the largest/heaviest bead at the bottom. Be sure to leave at least ¾" of wire at the end of the pin. Holding the beads down to the bottom "head" of the pin in one hand, use the other hand to bend the end of the head-pin wire down just past a 90° angle.

Step 2: Using your rosary pliers, grasp the wire stem about ¼" from the bend. Roll the wire completely around the middle of the pliers, bringing the end of the wire back to its initial position.

Step 3: Holding the loop in place on the rosary pliers, use your fingers to wrap the end of the wire around the base of the loop. With the tip of your bent-nose pliers, tuck the end of the wire into place so that there are no points sticking out. Repeat steps if you are adding multiple bead drops to the keychain.

Step 4: Using your bent-nose pliers and rosary pliers, open the jump ring. Hook the jump ring through the loop on your bead drop and through the solid ring, then close the jump ring. Repeat this step for each bead drop if you are using multiples. Slide the solid ring onto the large split chain keyring.

CHARMS

Creating small bead charms with leftover beads allows you to customize some of your favorite jewelry pieces by adding in or swapping out different beads to coordinate with outfits and occasions.

MATERIALS TO GATHER
- Beads
- Head pins
- Small lobster-claw clasp

TOOLS
- Bead mat/rimmed tray for materials
- Rosary pliers
- Bent-nose or chain-nose pliers

MAKE IT!

Step 1: Lay out your bead design, stacking the bead(s) onto the head pins. If you are using multiple beads, use the largest/heaviest bead at the bottom. Be sure to leave at least ¾" of wire at the end of the pin. Bend the wire at a 90° angle against the bottom of the setting, leaving approximately ½" of wire past the bend.

Step 2: Using the wide base of your rosary pliers, roll the wire around the pliers to form a large loop. Place the wire end through the clasp. Using your fingertips, wrap the end of the wire around the base of the loop. With the tip of your bent-nose pliers, tuck the end of the wire into place so that there are no points sticking out.

> ### Pro Tip
> Fun, cheerful, and bright beads make especially fun charms. Add some extra interest to the design by adding in things like sparkly rhinestone rondelle spacers and mixed textures.

BOBBY PINS

• - • - • - • - • - • - •

Out of all the fun, surprisingly doable projects in this book, I have a feeling that this one may become one of your favorites (It's definitely one of mine!). There's something so sweet and fun about a customized bobby pin, especially with the unexpected addition of some beautiful beads.

MATERIALS TO GATHER
- 2–4mm beads
- 1 (24–26-gauge) wire, approximately 6"–8" long
- Bobby pins

TOOLS
- Bead mat/rimmed tray for materials
- Bent-nose or chain-nose pliers
- Cutters

MAKE IT!
Step 1: Lay out your bead design, making sure your beads will fit along the bobby pin without excess hangover (smaller beads will work best for this project).

Step 2: Loop one end of the wire through the end of the bobby pin, wrapping one end of the wire back around itself 2 to 3 times. Use the tip of your bent-nose pliers to tuck the end of the wire in smoothly.

Step 3: Add a bead onto the wire, positioning the bead so that it sits on top of the bobby pin. Holding the bead in place, wrap the end of the wire around the top arm of the bobby pin, bringing it up on the other side. Add on another bead, repeating this step until you get to the end of the bobby pin.

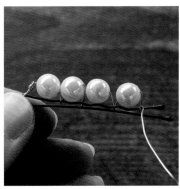

(Continued on next page)

Step 4: Wrap the end of the wire around the end of the bobby pin arm 3 to 4 times to secure the beads. Use your cutters to trim the end of the wire, then tuck in the end of the wire using the tip of your bent-nose pliers. (I like to tuck the end of the wire into the end bead to ensure no sharp edges are out.)

Pro Tip
Cut a square of some pretty card stock and slip three bobby pins onto one end for a sweet, simple, and memorable gift.

BOOKMARKS

Bookmarks are one of those things that you don't really know you need until you have one, and once you do, you find you need about a dozen of them. This project calls for beading at both ends of the bookmark, but if your books are shelved on-end you can modify to adorn only one end.

MATERIALS TO GATHER

- Velvet or grosgrain ribbon
- Beads
- Ribbon clamp ends (make sure the clamp is about wide as the ribbon)
- Superglue
- Beads
- Head pins
- Jump rings

TOOLS

- Bead mat/rimmed tray for materials
- Cutters/scissors
- Bent-nose pliers
- Nylon-jaw pliers (optional)
- Rosary pliers

MAKE IT!

Step 1: Cut your ribbon to the desired length (10" is the length I use, as that seems to fit most of the books in my collection). Open the ribbon clamp end and add a small dot of superglue. Insert one end of the ribbon into the ribbon clamp end, making sure to push the ribbon all the way to the angle of the clamp. Using the flat edge of your bent-nose pliers, gently squeeze the clamp closed. If your ribbon clamp has a smooth finish, you can use nylon-jaw pliers or a small piece of soft cloth or leather between the clamp and your bent-nose pliers when squeezing the clamp closed.

(Continued on next page)

Step 2: Holding the beads down to the bottom "head" of the pin in one hand, use the other hand to bend the end of the head-pin wire down just past a 90° angle. Using your rosary pliers, grasp the wire stem about ¼" from the bend. Roll the wire completely around the middle of the pliers, bringing the end of the wire back to its initial position.

Step 3: Holding the loop in place on the rosary pliers, use your fingers to wrap the end of the wire around the base of the loop. With the tip of your bent-nose pliers, tuck the end of the wire into place so that there are no points sticking out. Repeat steps if you are using multiple bead drops in your project.

Step 4: Open the jump ring and add on the bead drops. Hook the end of the jump ring through the loop on the ribbon clamp end, then close the jump ring. If you are creating a double-sided bookmark, repeat steps for the other end of the ribbon.

Pro Tip

A double-ended ribbon bookmark is a beautiful addition to books that are stored on bedside tables or otherwise laying down. If your books are stored standing on-end, a single-ended bookmark will be the design you want.

ACKNOWLEDGMENTS

• • • • • • • • • • • •

There have been so many influential people who have walked with me through this long and winding path to becoming who I am today. The most influential person, though, was my dear Bubbie (grandmother) who was my best friend and self-proclaimed "#1 fan." Though Bubbie left this world in 2011, she remains in my heart and in the hearts of everyone who ever knew her. Without her as the family matriarch and my North Star, my life's path would have been quite different.

My dear husband Erik and sweet daughter Evelyn Agnes together make up our small but mighty family unit. They both offer me unconditional love and support, and without them I could not be who I am. Everything I do is for our family, and I love them both so much more than I could ever possibly convey in words.

My brother Alex has taught me that miracles are real, and anything is possible. Aunt Patti, my dear Godmother, is the quintessential renaissance woman and has shown me how to weave many seemingly unrelated talents together to create one wonderful life. Both Alex and Aunt Patti were essential not only to this project, but to my business and life as a whole.

My dear mother is the hardest working woman I know, and she has rallied behind me with unwavering support throughout all my crafty endeavors. My father, a wandering spirit, taught me that it's okay for your plan to be that you have no plan.

Sarah Ramberg, the incredible artist and creator behind Sadie Seasongoods and author of *Crafting with Flannel*, for being generous with sharing her time and opportunities.

My bestie, Jeanne, artist and creator at juNxtaposition, has been a mentor and friend to me since the moment we met ten-ish years ago. Her willingness to entertain my endless "I've got an idea" calls has given me the encouragement and support I needed to bring my business to where it is today.

All my friends, family, colleagues, customers, and anyone else who has played a part in my life, everything I do is possible because of you. Thank you.